Descendants of William Archibald Edwards

1. **WILLIAM ARCHIBALD**[1] **EDWARDS** was born on 28 Feb 1835 in Talbot County, Georgia. He died on 12 Dec 1926 in Dallas, Texas. He married Eliza Jones White, daughter of Theophilus White and Mary H. Jett on 05 Jan 1858 in Russell County, Alabama. She was born on 08 Apr 1836 in Meriwether County, Georgia. She died on 06 Sep 1922 in Dallas, Texas.

More About William Archibald Edwards:
Burial: 14 Dec 1926 in Oak Cliff Cemetery, Dallas,
Texas
Occupation: 1861; Farmer
Occupation: 1870 in Autauga County, Alabama; Minister
Occupation: 1880 in Farmersville, Texas; School Teacher
Occupation: 1900 in Eagle Ford, Dallas County, Texas; Minister
Occupation: 1910 in Dallas, Dallas County, Texas; Retired
Occupation: 1920 in Dallas, Dallas County, Texas; Retired - Living with his daughter Eliza and her husband George Cochran
Occupation: Methodist Minister
Military Service: Bet. 03 Jul 1861-13 Aug 1863 ; Company E, 15th Alabama Infantry, C.S.A.

Notes for William Archibald Edwards:
Letter to Rufus Painter

Dallas, Tex., Nov. 11,
1915.
Dear Ruf:
   I wrote you for a list of my dear old Co. E. 15th Alabama Regiment who are now living, and as you were sick Bro. Charley Edwards sent me the following list vis.-W.R. Painter, W.C. Mizell Ozark; J.R. Edwards, Mat Williams, Ariton; C. V. Atkinson, Newton; Newt Curenton, Haw Ridge; Albert Austin, Daleville; W.D. Byrd, B.W. Fleming, Enterprise; Dorse Fleming, Geneva; C.G. Dillard, Ozark Route 1. To this I add the Texas list---Capt. Wm. A. Edwards, 4019 Bowser St. Dallas Texas; A.N. Edwards, Gordon, Tex.;Y.M. Edwards, Alvin, Tex.; J.P. Martin, Italy, Tex.; Ben Martin, Waxahachie, Tex.; Wm. Mobly Crandal Dallas County, Tex. The above constitute the list of survivors as I have it. If you know of any others please add them to this.
   The Company left home with 84 men enlisted all told 200. Returned home after surrender 100. So you see 100 brave and as good men as Dale or any other county ever raised sleep in some Northern or Southern cemetery or in shallow crude graves on some battle field, or possibly some were buried under the winter snow or to decay on some bloody hard fought battle ground and their bones to bleach under a burning sun, and to their dust and memory we say farewell dear comrades, and we hope some day to meet you beyond the flash and roar of artillery and rattle of musketry.
   It will probably be some interest to the friends and survivors of Co. E. to read a short write up of the Company which I hope you will have the Star to publish and send a copy to all living members. I t will likely be the last message they will ever get from me as I am now past eighty and they are not in their teens. I want each to take this as a personal letter and I would be glad to have a letter from all of them.
   No better Co. of citizen soldiers ever left any community than left Westville on the 18th day of July 1861, 54 years ago the past July. No more sumptuous feast was ever spread for departing patriots than was spread under the shade of the beautiful oaks that stood around old Darian Church. The loving hands that prepared it have long since been wafted beyond the curse of war and rage of battles by the angels of God. In all my life I have never seen deeper and purer emotions or heard so tender farewells as followed that sumptuous feast. Husbands and wives embraced in tender love and with many it was the last embrace---fathers kissed their only babes--- mothers threw a mothers arm around her son and with a mothers deep prayer sent her soldier boy to the conflict of battle and perils of war. And some of the boys felt the tender touch of the bride-to-be as they

clasped hands that day. It thrilled their souls and nerved their arm for deeds of daring until they either perished in the campaign or returned home under the furled banner of the Stars and Bars. I have often been anxious to know if any of them that got back got left. "That day many parted, Where few shall meet."

That night we camped at Fraziers mill on Pea river and almost the entire company took a bath, and if there were either snakes, alligators or varmints for miles around they took to the hills and swamps never to return. Such a babel of voices and splashing of water I have never heard. The next night we camped in the open streets of Perote, and its bests families welcomed us with royal favors, and our third night out we stopped at Union Springs and spent the Sabbath there, which stay will always be kindly remembered by Co.E. That was the day of the first Manassas battle and Bull Run episode. Many thought the war was ended and some kind hearted mothers hoped their boys might see Richmond before they were disbanded. Well the boys saw Richmond and beyond. How little we knew of war and the bitter cup before the South.

We next find ourselves organized as Co. E. in the 15th Alabama Regiment. Nothing of special interest to the Co. E until our regiment camped at Camp Toombs between Centerville and Manassas. There Dick Neil died. This is worthy of mentioning because he was the first member of Co. E that died and the first one that had died in a regimental camp. He was honored as but few soldiers are ever honored. The Regiment was drawn up to witness the solemn burial, and Co. E with reversed arms and muffled drum followed the corpse to the road that leads from Centerville to Manassas; and there in a plain coffin with a soldiers blanket for a winding sheet we buried him and a platoon of Co. E fired a soldier salute about the lonely grave, and there on the lonely spot unmarked by human hands and unknown to the busy world that passes that way to-day sleeps the dust of Corporal Neil without a stain on his name or character at home or in the army. It was the first crude shock that came to Co. E and it threw a gloom over the folks at home as nothing had done. All began to realize that war was on, and I remember at that camp Col. Canty told me it would be a terrible struggle. We spent the winter at Manassas and the only thing of special interest to Co. E was the task of getting boards for winter quarters, a task I never heard a single member complain of.

I was sent with my Company across Bull Run to the east of Centerville in the hilly and wooded country that had been but little occupied by soldiers up to that time, to get boards to cover huts for winter quarters. And old federal sympathizer lived about half a mile from our camp and killed hogs one day, it would have been better had he killed all he had. I went up to his house and wanted to buy a hasslet. He asked 50 cents for it and at that time we thought ten or fifteen cents good pay. I went back where the boys were at work and related what had occurred and I saw one of them give a significant wink and asked "Do you love hasslet Captain and I told him yes." Well to make a long story short, next morning when I woke up there was a ham of a 250 pound hog slipped under my tent and a large hasslet hanging in front and John Trawick, my cook, singing, whistling and frying liver and ham just as happy as he could get and you remember John could get very happy. I ate it and asked no questions for conscience sake, and as well as I remember it was the first and last stolen meat I ate during the war.

1862 was the fighting year of the war. Before the ground had thawed and the buds had burst into leaves we were taken from our pleasant quarters and transferred to the valley and received a formal introduction to Stonewall Jackson. There are two incidents in this campaign I wish to relate, not battles the historian does that, but unnoticed and unknown to the historian yet of interest to the Co. E. I allude to the death of Jno. Trawick and Lieut. Mills. John Trawick was killed almost under the guns of Harpers Ferry, when we halted in our pursuit of Banks. We were resting on the turn-pike when a gun accidentally discharged and shattered poor Johns heel to pieces. He was carried to a Winchester Hospital, and in a few days I received notice he was dead.

I want to say this for John Trawick, I detailed him to cook for me, and he did more for my comfort than any one else has ever done. He carried my luggage on marches. (He was big and strong.) When the Regiment halted, if it was mid-night he spread my bedding and cooked my supper no matter how tired he was, and I have often wondered if Israel's chariot was sent down to take that rough, rugged yet noble son of nature to a bright and better world.

Lieut. Mills was killed at Cross Keys, when an unexpected retreat was ordered our regiment. He was a hightoned, brave Christian gentlemen confided in at home and honored and loved in the army. He was devoted to his mess and his mess to him, quiet, intelligent, refined and dignified, a high type of a Christian gentleman yet he always impressed me that a cloud was over his spirits and I have never thought he expected to survive the war, and I thought and still think that terrible specter of presentment was ever before his eyes.

At night after the terrible battle of Gains Mills at Richmond after night fall had covered the field of carnage and death which was strewed with dead and dying, I fell on Billy Robinson, a fine specimen of manhood, tall, angular swarthy, hair as black as a crow and fearless as a lion. He told me he was mortally wounded and could live but a little while. He asked me who held the field I told him we held it. Then he said I am willing to die. Tell father I died fighting for my home and country, that I died brave and I feel I am prepared for a better world. His father was a Methodist preacher.

Co. E did the fighting for Hood's division at Suffolk. It held the line against great odds early morning till night, did the picket duty till mid night and covered the retreat of the army twenty or twenty five miles to Black Water River. I doubt if any Company ever withstood so strong and persistent attack, more courageously and firmly than did Co. E. A whole brigade against one company for an entire day, but we had the position on them.

During the engagement I met Jess Flowers, hat off, sleeves rolled up, and sweat rolling from his brow. He said Captain they have killed my mess mate Cameron, and I am ready to fight the whole Yankee army. I believe Jess would have tried it. Cameron was a good man and soldier and died with his face to the enemy. The only three men I detailed to cook for me were Trawick, Flowers and Charley Jones; the first two were killed and Charley Jones crippled for life.

While we were at Suffolk, the battle of the wilderness was fought and fighting Joe Hooker whipped. Thence we followed Lee to Gettysburg, which with the surrender of Fort Donaldson sealed the fate of the Confederacy. They first brought Grant, the man of destiny, into the lime light, and second, settled the question of invasion, and so reduced Lee's army that it was only a question of time when it would succumb to superior force. But I wish to say a few things about that great and fatal battle. First the 15th, Alabama went further in that battle than any other troop, second Co. E went as far as any part of the Regiment and staid as long. The men fired their guns until the barrels become so hot they could not hold and load them.

The death of private Holloway was to me the saddest feature of this sanguinary struggle. We were well protected behind a great rock about 4 feet high, the enemy equally protected behind a rock fence not more than 50 yards in front of us, and Captain Park reported a flanking division (Sickles) coming in our rear. Col. Oates ordered a charge and mounted the rock himself and discharged the contents of a six shooter in the face of the enemy. No one would follow but Holloway who mounted the rock, fell on his left knee, fixed his musket and a ball from the enemy crashed through his left temple and he fell dead on the feet of his gallant Colonel. How gallant! How useless! I saw the gallant deed and in the rage of battle and reign of death I thought what a sorrow it would carry to the bereaved wife and ten orphaned children far away in our beloved Alabama.

But our hearts were not always heavy and our heads bowed with grief. The soldier out of battle was ready for favor and the evening before the Gettysburg battle Co. E. was out on the picket line.

Gen. Lee had ordered no private property disturbed and among the grove of large oaks in which we were camped a bunch of fine hogs had been browsing for acorns all day. Co. E's mouth had been watering all day for a taste of Yankee pork. Late that evening the Colonel told me there would be rations that evening and to let any one kill one of those hogs. I called the Co. together and told them to kill one of the biggest hogs and before I could stop them they had killed three and had a fourth so nearly dead I allowed them to finish it. But a very amazing thing occurred during the hog killing. I had two men in my Company, some of you may still remember them for no Company could well be without two such men. One was Sam Hog, a great big over grown man, and Peters a small little fellow, and I looked out and saw Peters coming towards me closely pursued by Hog, nearly in touching distance and at every leap he would cry "help me Captain! Help me Captain." I called a halt-inquired the trouble, Hog said Peters hit him with a rock and nearly broke his leg, and Peters gasping for breath said "Captain you told us to kill the biggest hog we could find and he was the biggest one I saw. It was so ludicrous Hog burst into loud laughter and, limping, turned to his quarters. The truth was Peters had missed his mark.

One more incident that was very amusing to me, and the strange part is it never cease to be amusing to me. The parties to this incident were uncle Dave Snell and Latimer, both as true and worth men as ever girded their shoes with the accentments of war or shouldered a musket, both are now under the soil beyond the din of battle.

One morning at roll call Latimer came up with a broken arm and it was broken after the rest of the Company had gone to bed, Uncle Dave was to report the case and with the usual gravity of old men. He said he and Latimer went to the spring to get water to cook and coming up from the spring with a bucket of water his foot slipped, he fell and broke his arm. No one dared question Uncle Dave's word, but it seemed strange to me they should be out at midnight after water to cook, I said nothing knowing full well if it had any rich or racy features the boys could not keep it from me. So I pretty soon got a full statement of the case, and not very much like Uncle Dave's. They had gone to a nearby apple orchard and Latimer climbed a tree and sized a hornets nest and in his hasty retreat a limb broke, he fell and broke his arm. A few days after on the march I asked the old soldier to tell me exactly how the accident occurred and with great precision he related the affair to where Latimer started up the hill with his camp kettle of water and said "Captain he got slickest fall I ever saw." Well says I, Uncle Dave were there any hornets about the spring. "Captain" he said "I'll tell you all about it". I told him no I knew it all. I never blamed him, only Latimer for not knowing the difference between an apple and a hornet nest. In fact I never blamed Adam so much for eating that red apple Eve gave him, I expect I would have done as he did. This occurred as well as I remember at Raccoon ford of the Rapidan.

In conclusion of this article to my old true and tried friends and comrades-friends and soldiers tried in the crucible of fire. There are a few things I reflect on with great pleasure.

1st, after the surrender Co. E returned from the scenes of battle and war, with true manhood and moral character and honest purpose entered honorable business and have been successful and useful citizens.

2nd, that my original mess eight of us are still living and constitute nearly half of the now living members of the Company.

3rd, and last and by far the most pleasing reflection is that I treated my Company as gentlemen, They were gentlemen at home and I could see no reason why they should not be treated as gentlemen in the army and I do not remember having punished one of my men, I consciously believed discipline could be maintained without it, and I do not believe the Confederacy ever produced a better Company on the march a more orderly one in camps, nor a braver one in battle, and soon the last of us will hear the tattoo for final sleep and rest, and the reveille. When the trumpet of God shall awake and the sleeping dust of earths millions, and may we answer the roll call on that side of the river that makes glad the city of God.

Wm. A. EDWARDS

First Lieutenant July 3, 1861; Captain March 6, 1862; Resigned September 2, 1863 and served as Chaplain for the duration of the War.

Enlisted on July 3, 1861 at Fort Mitchell, Alabama and served until resigning to become Chaplain on September 2, 1863.

Engagements: Winchester, Cross Keys, Cold Harbor, Fredericksburg, Suffolk, Hazel River, 2nd Manassas, Chantilly, Harpers Ferry, Sharpsburg, Shepardstown, Gettysburg, Battle Mount.

Pre War residence was Westville, Alabama.

June 3-August 1, 1863 -- The Gettysburg Campaign.
No. 444.--Report of Col. William C. Oates, Fifteenth Alabama Infantry.

AUGUST 8, 1863.

SIR: I have the honor to report, in obedience to orders from brigade headquarters, the participation of my regiment in the battle near Gettysburg on the 2d ultimo.
My regiment occupied the center of the brigade when the line of battle was formed. During the advance, the two regiments on my right were moved by the left flank across my rear, which threw me on the extreme right of the whole line. I encountered the enemy's sharpshooters posted behind a stone fence, and sustained some loss thereby. It was here that Lieut. Col. Isaac B. Feagin, a most excellent and gallant officer, received a severe wound in the right knee, which caused him to lose his leg. Privates (A.) Kennedy, of Company B, and (William) Trimner, of Company G, were killed at this point, and Private (G. E.) Spencer, Company D, severely wounded.

After crossing the fence, I received an order from Brigadier-General Law to left-wheel my regiment and move in the direction of the heights upon my left, which order I failed to obey, for the reason that when I received it I was rapidly advancing up the mountain, and in my front I discovered a heavy force of the enemy. Besides this, there was great difficulty in accomplishing the maneuver at that moment, as the regiment on my left (Forty-seventh Alabama) was crowding me on the left, and running into my regiment, which had already created considerable confusion. In the event that I had obeyed the order, I should have come in contact with the regiment on my left, and also have exposed my right flank to an enfilading fire from the enemy. I therefore continued to press forward, my right passing over the top of the mountain, on the right of the line. On reaching the foot of the mountain below, I found the enemy in heavy force, posted in rear of large rocks upon a slight elevation beyond a depression of some 300 yards in width between the base of the mountain and the open plain beyond. I engaged them, my right meeting the left of their line exactly. Here I lost several gallant officers and men.

After firing two or three rounds, I discovered that the enemy were giving way in my front. I ordered a charge, and the enemy in my front fled, but that portion of his line confronting the two companies on my left held their ground, and continued a most galling fire upon my left.
Just at this moment, I discovered the regiment on my left (Forty-seventh Alabama) retiring. I halted my regiment as its left reached a very large rock, and ordered a left-wheel of the regiment, which was executed in good order under fire, thus taking advantage of a ledge of rocks running off in a line perpendicular to the one I had just abandoned, and affording very good protection to my men. This position enabled me to keep up a constant flank and cross fire upon the enemy, which in less than five minutes caused him to change front. Receiving reinforcements, he charged me five times, and was as often repulsed with heavy loss. Finally, I discovered that the enemy had flanked me on the right, and two regiments were moving rapidly upon my rear and not 200 yards distant, when, to save my regiment from capture or destruction, I ordered a retreat. Having become exhausted from fatigue and the excessive heat of the day, I turned the command of the regiment over to Capt. B. A. Hill, and instructed him to take the men off the field, and reform the regiment and report to the brigade.

My loss was, as near as can now be ascertained, as follows, to wit: 17 killed upon the field, 54 wounded and brought off the field, and 90 missing, most of whom are either killed or wounded. Among the killed and wounded are 8 officers, most of whom were very gallant and efficient men.

Recapitulation.--Killed, 17; wounded, 54; missing, 90; total, 161.

I am, lieutenant, most respectfully, your obedient servant,

W. C. OATES,
Colonel, Commanding Fifteenth Alabama Regiment

Lieut. B.O. PETERSON,
Acting Assistant Adjutant-General

See "NOTES" for Eliza Jones White for William Archibald Edwards autobiography.

More About Eliza Jones White:
d: 06 Sep 1922 in Dallas, Texas
Burial: 08 Sep 1922 in Oak Cliff Cemetery, Dallas, Texas

Notes for Eliza Jones White:
Oak Cliff Cemetery records give first name as "Elvira".

Autobiography
Or some incidents in my life by Reverend William A. Edwards
Pate, Texas, 1897

I was born in Talbot County, Georgia on the 28th day of February, 1835. The day is designated in history as the cold Friday. It was the coldest day in the history of that country up to that date and I am sure that it has never been equaled since. It was said that the freeze was so powerful and deep that great trees of the forest burst and many of them died.

My father's name was Ambrose Edwards. He lived to be eighty-two years of age. My grandfather's name was William Edwards. He died at the age of eighty-four. I think he was born in the eastern part of Virginia and my impression is that he was the son of Ambrose Edwards.

My grandmother Edwards was Mary Whatley. I know very little of her family. I never saw any near kin on my grandmother's side of the house.

My father had a house built on his farm to take care of his parents in their old age. They had not occupied it more than a month before my grandmother died and grandfather then lived with his children, making his home with his youngest son, William Edwards.

My grandfather made a profession of religion and received the sacrament on his deathbed. My father, Ambrose Edwards, joined the Methodist Church at the age of twenty-five years and was one of the best men I ever knew.

My mother was Emeline James Gaulding, the daughter of John Gaulding. She died at the age of seventy-six. My grandfather Gaulding died of yellow fever in Mobile, Alabama when about sixty years old.

I never knew my grandmother Gaulding's maiden name or Christian name. I remember very distinctly seeing my father returning from the post office handing my mother a letter notifying her of the death of her father and the deep grief it produced on her refined and emotional nature. Mother died in her seventy-seventh year and both were buried in Westville, Dale County, Alabama.

My Edwards ancestors were robust in mind and body; were not afraid of anything; they nearly all acquired good property, but none of my father's family took much to books. On the other hand, my mother was a cultivated woman, about as much so as any raised in her day. The Gaulding family was cultivated and intelligent. Archibald Gaulding, the uncle for whom "A" in my name stands, was one of Georgia's most intelligent citizens. He was the most fascinating gentleman I nearly ever knew, as neat as a pin, as handsome as Absalom, as polite as Chesterfield, thoroughly educated, he was a man of mark. He served his state in the legislature, was a candidate for governor, but defeated, was for two terms auditor of the state road, and for many years, the State Masonic Lecturer and considered the brightest Mason in the state.

I received my strong bodily constitution from the Edwards side and whatever taste or acquirements I may have in literature comes from my mother's family. I believe that my general knowledge exceeds that of any of my Edwards kin with whom I have met.

At the age of 14 I professed religion at Shady Grove Church in Lee County, Alabama. With my conversion came a clear call to the ministry, neither of which I have ever since doubted.

On the morning of the 5th day of January, 1858 I married Eliza Jones Mizell, the widow of James S. Mizell, and daughter of Theophilus White. We have raised eight children to be grown, two boys and six girls, all of them married. We have 27 grandchildren, six of which died, and as we grow older our life becomes more unified and happy. The names of our children are, respectfully:

Theophilus Ambrose Edwards
Mary James Cora (Mrs. J. A. Skillern)
Annie Lee (Mrs. S. N. Neathery)
Willie Maud (Mrs. T. B. Lester)
Mattie Elizabeth (Mrs. B. L. Jones)
Carrie Louise (Mrs. J. L. Wilson)
Eliza (Lida) Emeline (Mrs. Geo.B.Cochran)
William Archibald Edwards, Jr.

There were no events in my childhood of unusual interest, I was considered forward, egotistical, and full of pranks and mischief, and a superabundance of life.

I cared little for books until my conversion and union with the church. From that day until the present books have been my best and most constant companion.

It seems to me now I must have been a boy of unusual endurance. I used to pick cotton all day and then hunt possums and coons with father's Negroes nearly all night. The first money I ever had was twenty-five cents and I paid it all for a money purse and then wore the purse out carrying it in my pocket and never had a cent to put in it. I next made fifty cents and bought a pistol with that and one day all left home but me and I spent the entire day shooting chickens and never hit one. I then swapped the pistol for an old vest and mother wouldn't let me wear it. That ended the speculation.

I felt the call to the ministry from the day of my conversion and I suppose I have made some of what the world would call sacrifices to preach. My uncle, for whom I was named, offered to give me a legal profession if I would accept it, but I felt I must preach. When I entered the ministry I was offered a law partnership with a guarantee of $2.500.00 for the first year with every prospect of a large increase and yet I declined it to enter the ministry and I am now at the age of sixty-two more than pleased with my choice. The lawyer that made the offer was in one of two years killed by a stroke of lightning and had I accepted the offer, some ill fatality might have befallen me ere this.

I supposed my war record will interest my family more than my ministry as the family is familiar with the latter.

Early in the summer of sixty one I raised a company of volunteers, went to the war as its first lieutenant and was soon promoted to captain in which capacity I served until near the close of the war and received the appointment of missionary to the soldiers, resigned and came home. The immediate cause of my resignation was the promotion of Major Lowther to the Colonelcy, a man I had refused to serve under.

We left home for Virginia the 21st day of June. The day after the Battle of Bull Run was fought; we rendezvoused at the Ft. Mitchell near Columbus, Georgia and was organized in the 15th Alabama regiment as Company "E" and when we reached Virginia was placed in Trumble's Brigade, Ewell's Division, Army of Northern Virginia. Law afterward commanded the brigade and General J. B. Hood the division. We were under General Jackson in all of his valley campaigns and cooperated with Lee against McClellan in the seven days fight around Richmond. General Jackson's forces came from the Valley and struck to the rear of the Federal Army at Mechanicsville, six miles north of Richmond. In this battle General Ewell, I think, saved Lee's army from being routed by his presence and bravery. The confederates had almost fallen into a panic when the brave old man, with hat in hand, headed the retreating men crying at the top of his voice: "Men for God's sake, fight. You must fight, you must fight."

His presence and cheering words acted like magic. His men rallied a well nigh lost battle. I have never seen this stated in history, yet I always thought this saved the day. There were some incidents of this battle too pathetic not to mention. We slept that night on the battlefield, among the dead and dying. In wandering about in the dark to look for my men I stumbled on a dead man and by some strange impulse I stooped, passed my hand over his face and recognized him to be Andrew Wilson, a young man who had boarded at my father's and taught school. I called for a light, searched his person and found on him a fine gold watch and $2.00 in silver, which I sent home to his parents. I also found a cousin, his name was Carlisle, a noble youth and I always thought one of the most handsome men I ever saw. A minie ball had entered his left lung. He was sitting up with his head bowed forward and over and anon, the gurgling sound told the sad tale that life was rapidly passing away. He was suffering intensely. I asked him if he knew me. He said "It's Cousin Billie". I asked him if I could help him and he muttered rather indistinctly "water". I took a canteen of water from a dead man and I held it to his mouth and he drank freely of it. I saw all was over with him, that I could do no more for him. I left him to struggle alone in the dark with none to soothe or comfort and I have always indulged the hope that an angel carried his noble and brave soul beyond the conflict of armies and the cruelty of war.

There was yet another touching incident in this night ramble among the dead. I had a private soldier, W. C. Robinson, in my Company. He was the son of an old itinerant Methodist preacher of the Alabama Conference. I called out "15 Alabama" and not far off he answered, "here". I asked "Is this you Billy?" He said, "Yes". I said, "Are you much hurt?" He replied, "I am killed." I found a minie ball had passed through his body and that his statement was too true. He said, "Who holds the battlefield". He faced danger with the chivalry of the bravest knight and death with the placidity of the bravest Christian.

I was on the battleground ten days after the battle. No Federal soldiers had been buried. They were in a state of putrefaction and were distended almost to the condition of bursting. Thousands of these poor fellows lay on the ground, in some places I could have walked for hundreds of yards on the dead and Federal troops had turned as black as a Negro which they invariably did in a few hours after they were killed. It was a phenomenon the Confederates did not turn black. This was not only a dreary, revolting spectacle, but seen just at night, was a frightful sight.

I saw an old excavation cut in a railroad with hundreds of Yankee soldiers killed together not covered with earth.

The confederates had been buried, but in a small clump of oak trees I found one confederate soldier. Evidently he had been dead but a few hours and, no doubt, he died from neglect and starvation. I paused, looked at the little pile of bones mess emaciated manhood and in the sympathy of my soul said here lies a noble dead, perhaps brave and good and yet no marble slab will ever mark his resting place and no wife or mother will ever learn of his painful and lingering death.

The battleground was under a flag of truce and that night I slept in some house with at least a dozen volunteers and army surgeons.

We waded the Potomac River to get to the Battle of Gettysburg and returning crossed on pontoons. There are some facts in this battle I have not seen in history. The 15th Alabama Regiment was the extreme right of General Lee's. Just as we began the attack Hood was wounded and Law took command of the division. Our regiment crept over Little Round Top Mountain and fought until all our ammunition was exhausted and for want of reinforcement and ammunition was compelled to retire.

In this battle I saw General Bulger shot through the body. He fell like a dead man and after the war I met the same gentleman. He was a candidate for Governor of the State of Alabama.

I saw Colonel Oates, since Governor of Alabama, mount a rock within thirty yards of the enemy and discharge the contents of a repeater in their face.

When we began the retreat back across the mountains the Federals were pressing and I was exhausted and with my third lieutenant and private soldier, slipped into a cave in the side of the mountain and about midnight came out, located the pickets by the firing and crowded between their post which was about a hundred yards apart and reached our command in safety. I am satisfied I went as far toward Washington as any other Southern soldier.

On many of our campaigns we often waded rivers from waist to neck deep and that we might stem the current we walked, four abreast, and with arms around each other, constituted mutual support. I had a very narrow escape at Suffolk on the southern side of Richmond. I was in command of a long line of pickets and had the advantage of a dense line of timber that covered us from view of the enemy. The line was at least eight hundred yards long and my left wing gave way while I was at the right and I ran in between my own men and the enemy who had then entered the woods and had driven my forces back. I found myself within a hundred yards of a solid line of Federal Soldiers, but as the woods were dense I do not think they ever saw me. I found my command had secured a good position about five hundred yards back and quietly awaited my coming.

The army began its retreat at dark and I was left on duty with orders to withdraw at one A.M. sharp and cover the retreat to Black Water, twenty-five miles, which I did without loss of a man and in perfect order. In that fight I lost several of my best men. One soldier whose name was Cameron was killed and my detailed cook, Jesse Flowers, carried him back to camp and his body now rests in an old pine thicket near Suffolk, Virginia. Flowers met me on his return with his sleeves rolled up to his elbows and said, "Captain, they have killed my old mess mate and best friend and I am now ready to fight until they kill me or I kill some of them." Soon the news came to me that Jesse Flowers was killed. By the side of his friend they buried him. Two braver soldiers never shouldered a musket or wore the Confederate gray. I wish I could indulge in the hope that they might arise with the just. But Flowers was wicked and Cameron, I think, was not religious, so I throw the mantle of oblivion over these two men and await the revelation of the great hereafter.

The three best friends I had in the army or ever had, all met their death in the same way. One was Lieutenant Patten who took camp fever at Manassas in 1861 and was transferred to a hospital at Richmond and soon I received notice he was dead. He was a gentleman of intelligence and a friend that never faltered or flickered. When he left I felt like I should never see him again and too soon my forebodings were realized. He was a wicked man and the last word I ever heard from him before the final farewell was an oath. It is probable he may have had a death bed repentance and from his narrow and crude little bunk gone up to a wider and better berth.

The second was John Trawick. I detailed him as a cook. He was shot accidentally in the foot in the valley near Harper's Ferry and died in a hospital at Winchester. John Trawick was a poor man, illiterate, unmannerly, profane and dissipated and yet he would do more for me and my comfort than any man living or dead. After the hardest wars and battles he would never sleep, though we might not reach camp until 12 or 1 o'clock at night, until he had prepared my supper, no matter how I protested. I am ashamed to say after the lapse of thirty years how much Mr. Trawick did for me.

Florence was the third and as I have already spoken freely of him, I will let that suffice.

My work as missionary was to the troops of Florida. My headquarters were scattered from the mouth of the Sewanee River to St. Andrews Bay, from Marian to the nearest point on the coast was from fifty to sixty miles and there was but one human habitation between.

I took my wife and oldest child on one trip. We stayed all night at the midway house. It was a pole hut, twelve by fourteen; one room, besides my family there was another family of eleven persons and I have never yet found out how we all slept as the night was cold. One thing I remember, the man took quite a fancy to Mrs. Edwards and gave her a fine venison ham as we returned home.

There were many dense thickets or "Tight Eye Swamps" in all that country and served as an impregnable fortress for hostile deserters. I never passed one of these that I did not feel I was in great danger. I expected to hear the deserters' rifles from these thickets every time I passed them. I suffered far more uneasiness than I did in the regular army.

Returning from one of my tours to the post at St. Andrews Bay I met an army composed of Yankees, Negroes and deserters, they raided Marian, burned a part of the town and killed some of its citizens. It was ten miles out when they leveled their guns on me. I thought as I had no weapon and was outnumbered I had better surrender. They carried me ten miles further towards the coast and then took my horse, the best one I ever owned, and turned me loose on foot with a pair of heavy saddle pockets and seventy miles from home and twenty from anywhere else. On foot I started home. Almost the entire way was either exposed to danger from the deserters or Negroes loafing around, whose owners had run out of the country and they were imprudently occupying it.

In going from my home in south Alabama to the troops in Florida I had a stopping place with a Mrs. Clark. One evening just before sundown I met her and her little girl about two miles from her house. She told me I had better turn back that 300 deserters were camped at her house and they would either kill or badly mistreat me if I went on. I asked her if she could take care of me, she said she would try. I turned, rode back to her sister's and they held a consultation and decided to send or carry me to Mrs. Reed's, a deserter's wife, who lived in the lone pine woods back from the public road. These ladies said if the deserters came to Mrs. Reed's she would claim me as her guest and save me. Mrs. Reed agreed to take me and do the best she could for me. She lived in a pole cabin with open cracks as large as your arm. She fed me that night on boiled sweet potatoes, which was the best she had and all she had for my horse was peas. It was a bright moonlight night, here was a brilliant fire of lightwood on the hearth and I sat leaning back by a large crack in the chimney corner. I looked out and saw a line of deserters at least a hundred armed with shotguns and muskets coming right to my back. I asked the lady if it would not be safer if I moved. She said that would create suspicion and cause them to stop and if I did not move they would most likely pass on. I don't think I ever sat so still before or since or covered so little space. That night they attacked the county seat, Newton, fifteen miles away. Four were killed and so many wounded.

After the surrender there were marauders robbing and hanging men friendly to the war and supposed to have money and I had been told I would share a similar fate. So we gave our valuables to our cook, Hogue, among other things a $150.00 gold watch and I took a Negro boy, Lewis, a bed quilt and shotgun and went out in a thicket near the house determined if they came to have the advantage of being on the outside. After we had been up for about an hour I said, "Lewis, I will go to sleep and you watch and if anybody comes you wake me." "Yes, sah, Marse Billy, if any man hurts you this night he will have to first walk over my dead body."

I went to sleep and woke the next morning with Lewis sleeping by my side, enjoying a full share of the quilt with me. I never asked Mrs. Edwards how she spent the night, but I guess she was as good to the cook as I was to Lewis. This was the last uneasy night I ever spent on account of war.

The last transaction I ever had in Confederate money I sold a calf skin for $300.00.

I was, at one time, offered a position on the weather bureau with a salary of $1,500.00 and the rank of captain if I would be mustered into service. I declined it. There were times when I had flattering prospects as a preacher, but that is all gone now. I once had offers and temptations to other pursuits, but that is all gone.

An Arab once rode a fine horse in front of an English officer and the Englishman offered him such tempting prices for his animal he galloped away from it to get out of his reach.

So I have gone out of the way of temptations. I have not done it as the Arab, but Old Time has mounted me and has rode me beyond the flattering offers and temptations of the world and now I keep my eye on the mark for the prize of the high calling of God in Christ Jesus.

****

Thirty years have passed. I
am ninety years old today.
I have broken the family record.

My father died at 82 and my mother at 76, a pretty fair record for longevity. Besides my immediate family I have forty-five grandchildren.

One thing dominated me as far back as I can remember, a determination never to grow old, that is never to have old folk's ways, to be a boy in spirit through life and I do not think I have ever risen much above a boy in any respect. I suppose I have been what the world would call an optimist, that is, a man that hasn't anything and doesn't want anything. I think I had my duplicate in an old farmer in Alabama. He had forty acres at $3.00 per acre of land, and a possum dog and said he would not take forty thousand dollars for it. To me every picture of life has two sides and I have always turned the bright side to my gaze. I have always taken a forward look. The fate of Lot's wife early impressed me with the backward look.

I have preferred Paul's rule of action, forgetting the things that are behind.

Seventy-two years ago I joined the Methodist Church and my name was never off the church roll or the conference roll since.

I have been preaching sixty-four years and in all these years I have done many things I should not have done and left many things undone.

I think I can say today before the Good Father in whose presence I must soon appear I have always been loyal to Christ. I have confessed Him before me. I have taken the Christian side of every moral issue in life that has come before the public for action.

I joined the Alabama Conference and filled pastorates there as follows:
Central Institute, Autaugaville, Ivey Creek, Summerfield and Day. I remained in that conference ten years, then transferred to the North Texas Conference, November 17, 1875. Served the Sulphur Springs Circuit; and Greenville Station. Located in December, 1876. For several years I taught school near Greenville, 1876 to 1880. Farmersville, 1880 to 1884. Lewisville, 1884 to 1886.

In 1886 I was readmitted into the North Texas Conference. My pastoral charges were Collinsville, Mt. Pleasant, Atlanta, Kaufman, Wills Point, Cochran and Caruth, Royse City, Fate, West Dallas, Haskell Avenue and Princeton. Fifty years of my ministry was spent in Texas and thirty-five years of this time was spent preaching in and around Dallas. I have seen the M. E. Church South grow from 455,000 members to two and one quarter million.

On March 1, 1925, I was made Chaplain General of the Trans-Mississippi Department of the United Confederate Veterans which was a distinctive honor to me.
I am proud of my country, my church, and my family and the age in which I live.
****

My father passed away on December 12, 1926. He had reached the age of 91 years and 10 months.

He preached on his 90th birthday at the Oak Lawn Methodist Church on Cedar Springs and Oak Lawn Avenue.

On his 91st birthday, February 28, 1925, he preached at the Oak Cliff Methodist Church on Jefferson Street.

He was looking forward to preaching at the invitation of Dr. Gregory at First Methodist Church on the corner of Ross Avenue and Harwood on his 99th birthday.

He preached at Lakewood Methodist Church just one week before his death.

He was a frequent writer to the Texas Christian Advocate and to the Dallas Morning News.

A friend has said of him:

"Brother Edwards had all the charm of a cultured Christian gentleman. He was a reader of good books. He thought out the fundamental questions. He wrote with ease and always illuminatingly. He prepared thoroughly his own discourses and he expected the preacher to whom he listened to give a message of strength and clearness. He lived here far beyond the limit of most men, but he lived to the last with full purpose. He was loved and cherished in his own home and by his brethren and friends. He passed on to his glorious crown with God's grace, resting upon him and with peace and good will abounding towards all men. We shall see him again."

Mrs. George A.Cochran
2019 Bowser Avenue
Dallas,Texas

More About William Archibald Edwards and Eliza Jones White:
Marriage License: 04 Jan 1858 in Russell County, Alabama
Marriage Fact: Married by John C. Ardis, M.G.

William Archibald Edwards and Eliza Jones White had the following children:

2.   i. THEOPHILUS AMBROSE[2] EDWARDS was born on 17 Jul 1859 in Dale County, Alabama. He died on 11 Feb 1929 in Dallas, Texas. He married Nora Elizabeth Bumpass, daughter of William Presley Bumpass and Mariah Hungerford Thomas on 26 Dec 1882 in Collin County, Texas. She was born on 26 Sep 1858 in Sulphur Springs, Texas. She died on 19 Apr 1927 in Grand Prarie, Texas.

3.   ii. MARY JAMES CORA EDWARDS was born on 06 Sep 1864 in Dale County, Alabama. She died on 15 Jul 1935 in Bella Vista, Arkansas. She married James Arthur Skillern, son of William Franklin Skillern and Sarah Ann Henninger on 04 Nov 1884 in Lewisville, Texas. He was born on 29 May 1856 in Pikeville, Tennessee. He died on 29 Dec 1914 in Dallas, Texas.

4.   iii. ANNIE LEE EDWARDS was born on 08 Nov 1867 in Alabama. She died on 22 Apr 1908 in Haskell, Texas. She married Stephen Nathaniel Neathery, son of Allen Hill Neathery and Elizabeth Jemima Buie on 30 Dec 1884 in Denton County, Texas. He was born on 16 Jan 1864 in Texas. He died on 22 Nov 1943 in Haskell, Texas.

5.   iv. WILLIE MAUD EDWARDS was born on 22 Aug 1868 in Autauga County, Alabama. She died on 04 Aug 1946 in Dallas, Texas. She married Thomas Benton Lester on 03 Dec 1886 in Caddo, Indian Territory (Oklahoma). He was born on 29 Feb 1856 in Mississippi. He died on 13 Apr 1928 in Dallas, Texas.

6.   v. CARRIE LOUISE EDWARDS was born on 30 Sep 1871 in Autaugaville, Alabama. She died on 25 Nov 1971 in Albuquerque, New Mexico. She married James Lee Wilson, son of William Henry Wilson and Elizabeth C. Pickens on 27 Feb 1889 in Mt. Pleasant, Texas. He was born on 09 Mar 1863 in Franklin, Holmes County, Mississippi. He died on 23 Jan 1917 in Celina, Collin County, Texas.

7.　　vi. MATTIE ELIZABETH EDWARDS was born on 30 Sep 1871 in Autaugaville, Alabama. She died on 15 Oct 1969 in Dallas, Texas. She married Benjamin Lee Jones, son of William Edwards Jones and Lonette Holcombe on 27 Feb 1889 in Mt. Pleasant, Texas. He was born on 18 Mar 1862 in Collinsville, Texas. He died on 17 Sep 1937 in Dallas, Texas.

8.　　vii. ELIZA EMELINE EDWARDS was born on 09 Sep 1874 in Summerfield, Alabama. She died on 20 Jan 1964 in Dallas, Texas. She married George Henry Cochran, son of James Monroe Cochran and Margaret Lively on 30 Oct 1895 in Dallas, Texas. He was born on 04 Oct 1870 in Dallas, Texas. He died on 05 Apr 1956 in Dallas, Texas.

　　　viii. WILLIAM ARCHIBALD EDWARDS was born on 24 May 1876 in Greenville, Texas. He died on 22 Aug 1915 in Dallas, Texas. He married India May Hughes on 12 Jul 1899 in Atlanta, Texas. She was born on 21 Sep 1875 in Tennessee. She died on 29 Oct 1963.

More About William Archibald Edwards:
Burial: 24 Aug 1915 in Oak Cliff Cemetery, Dallas, Texas
Cause Of Death: Tuberculosis
Living In: 1910 Living with Frank and Elizabeth Skillern in Dallas, Texas.
Occupation: 1900 in Atlanta, Cass County, Texas; Commercial Traveller (Travelling Salesman)
Occupation: 1910 in Dallas, Dallas County, Texas; Travelling Salesman, American Soda Company

Generation 2

2.　**THEOPHILUS AMBROSE^2 EDWARDS** (William Archibald^1) was born on 17 Jul 1859 in Dale County, Alabama. He died on 11 Feb 1929 in Dallas, Texas. He married Nora Elizabeth Bumpass, daughter of William Presley Bumpass and Mariah Hungerford Thomas on 26 Dec 1882 in Collin County, Texas. She was born on 26 Sep 1858 in Sulphur Springs, Texas. She died on 19 Apr 1927 in Grand Prarie, Texas.

More About Theophilus Ambrose Edwards:
Burial: 13 Feb 1929 in Restland Memorial Park, Dallas, Texas
Cause Of Death: pneumonia
Occupation: 1900 in Ellis County, Texas; Cotton Broker
Occupation: 1910 in Dallas, Texas; Raw Cotton Exporter
Occupation: 1920 in Tarrant County, Texas; Farmer

More About Nora Elizabeth Bumpass:
Burial: Restland Memorial Park, Dallas, Texas

Theophilus Ambrose Edwards and Nora Elizabeth Bumpass had the following children:

9.　　i. CLARA LILLIAN^3 EDWARDS was born on 12 Feb 1884 in Farmersville, Texas. She died on 26 Oct 1973 in Ennis, Texas. She married Robert Roy Connally on 22 Sep 1904 in Waxahachie, Texas. He was born on 28 Sep 1881 in Ellis County, Texas.

10.　　ii. LAURA LEE OLIA EDWARDS was born on 09 Aug 1886 in Nevada, Texas. She died on 31 May 1981. She married Robert Weldford Troth on 17 Oct 1911 in Dallas, Texas. He was born on 20 Mar 1880 in Zachary, Louisiana. He died on 02 Feb 1951.

11.　　iii. THEOPHILUS MARVIN EDWARDS was born on 05 Sep 1888 in Farmersville, Texas. He died on 13 May 1969 in Dallas, Texas. He married Georgia Mae Barksdale on 12 Sep 1911 in Waxahachie, Texas. She was born on 27 Apr 1889 in Beckville, Texas. She died on 13 Apr 1986 in Dallas, Texas.

12.   iv. RUBY ELIZABETH EDWARDS was born on 15 Nov 1893 in Waxahachie, Texas. She died on 24 Sep 1966 in Dallas, Texas. She married Luther Price Robertson on 06 Oct 1924 in Arlington, Texas. He was born on 10 Oct 1893. He died on 25 Dec 1971.

3.   **MARY JAMES CORA[2] EDWARDS** (William Archibald[1]) was born on 06 Sep 1864 in Dale County, Alabama. She died on 15 Jul 1935 in Bella Vista, Arkansas. She married James Arthur Skillern, son of William Franklin Skillern and Sarah Ann Henninger on 04 Nov 1884 in Lewisville, Texas. He was born on 29 May 1856 in Pikeville, Tennessee. He died on 29 Dec 1914 in Dallas, Texas.

More About Mary James Cora Edwards:
Burial: Oak Cliff Cemetery, Dallas, Texas

More About James Arthur Skillern:
Burial: 30 Dec 1914 in Oak Cliff Cemetery, Dallas, Texas
Cause Of Death: Cancer
Living In: 1900 Oak Cliff, Dallas County, Texas
Living In: 1910 Dallas, Dallas County, Texas
Occupation: 1880 in Denton County, Texas; Drug Store Clerk
Occupation: 1896 in Dallas, Texas ; Founded Skillern Drug Store Chain with first Dallas Store.

James Arthur Skillern and Mary James Cora Edwards had the following children:

13.   i. WILLIAM ARTHUR[3] SKILLERN was born on 05 Aug 1885 in Lewisville, Texas. He died on 10 Jan 1922 in Dallas, Texas. He married Verna Lee Malone on 18 Jun 1907 in Dallas, Texas. She died on 20 Jul 1980.

14.   ii. FRANK LLOYD SKILLERN was born on 05 Aug 1886 in Lewisville, Texas. He died on 26 Jan 1917 in Dallas, Texas. He married Elizabeth Peyton on 01 Oct 1908. She was born about 1889 in Texas.

15.   iii. EDNA CORA SKILLERN was born on 31 Oct 1887 in Lewisville, Texas. She died on 21 Dec 1962 in Dallas, Texas. She married William Frank Cofer, son of Peter Joseph Cofer and Paulina Sawyer on 16 Apr 1912 in Dallas, Texas. He was born on 10 Mar 1884 in Illinois. He died on 13 Dec 1964 in Dallas, Dallas County, Texas.

16.   iv. LIDA SKILLERN was born on 15 Aug 1889 in Lewisville, Texas. She died on 29 Aug 1971 in Dallas, Texas. She married (1) CHARLES BASCOM PETERSON on 11 Apr 1911 in Dallas, Texas. She married C. K. CONE.

17.   v. RAE EDWARDS SKILLERN was born on 01 Nov 1894 in Sherman, Texas. He died on 15 Aug 1964 in Denton, Texas. He married Anne Wilson on 19 Nov 1913 in Dallas, Texas. She was born in 1894. She died on 15 Aug 1964.

18.   vi. ZULA SKILLERN was born on 27 Aug 1899 in Dallas, Texas. She died on 16 Sep 1983 in Dallas, Texas. She married John Vest Folsom, son of Samuel Christopher Folsom and Agnes Ann Traller on 11 Mar 1920 in Dallas, Texas. He was born on 11 Nov 1898 in Coryell County, Texas. He died on 18 Nov 1976.

19.   vii. ZOLA SKILLERN was born on 27 Aug 1899 in Dallas, Texas. She died on 01 Sep 1951 in Dallas, Texas. She married (1) WYLIE FONDREN WEATHERFORD, son of

William Eugene Weatherford and Alta Mary Gable on 29 Jul 1922 in Ferris, Texas. He was born on 20 Dec 1894 in Texas. He died on 31 Mar 1951 in Tarrant County, Texas. She married (2) THOMAS CHAPMAN F ERGUSON in Aug 1941. He was born on 18 Jul 1908 in Pennsylvania. He died on 16 Apr 1983 in Tarrant County, Texas.

20.   viii. MARY EVELYN SKILLERN was born on 15 Aug 1902 in Dallas, Texas. She died in Mar 1985 in Dallas, Texas. She married Leroy Monroe Napier, son of Leroy Munroe Napier on 10 Dec 1929. He was born on 19 Mar 1903. He died on 11 Jan 1969 in Dallas, Texas.

21.   ix. JEAN SKILLERN was born on 06 Dec 1906 in Dallas, Texas. She died on 17 Dec 1969. She married Robert Donald Hancock in 1932.

4.   **ANNIE LEE[2] EDWARDS** (William Archibald[1]) was born on 08 Nov 1867 in Alabama. She died on 22 Apr 1908 in Haskell, Texas. She married Stephen Nathaniel Neathery, son of Allen Hill Neathery and Elizabeth Jemima Buie on 30 Dec 1884 in Denton County, Texas. He was born on 16 Jan 1864 in Texas. He died on 22 Nov 1943 in Haskell, Texas.

More About Annie Lee Edwards:
Burial: Willow Cemetery, Haskell, Haskell County, Texas

More About Stephen Nathaniel Neathery:
Burial: 22 Nov 1943 in Willow Cemetery, Haskell, Haskell County, Texas
Cause Of Death: Heart Attack
Occupation: 1900 in Farmersville, Texas; Cotton Broker
Occupation: 1910 in Haskell, Haskell County, Texas; Cotton Broker
Occupation: 1920 in Haskell, Haskell County, Texas; Cotton Broker
Occupation: 1930 in Haskell, Haskell County, Texas; Retired
Occupation: 1940 in Haskell, Haskell County, Texas; Retired

Notes for Stephen Nathaniel Neathery:
Death Certificate gives January 20, 1864 as date of birth.

Stephen Nathaniel Neathery and Annie Lee Edwards had the following children:

22.   i. ORPHIE WILBUR[3] NEATHERY was born on 17 Oct 1885 in Farmersville, Texas. He died on 03 May 1953 in Mangum, Oklahoma. He married Connie Wills in Apr 1909 in Wichita Falls, Texas. She was born on 26 Feb 1887. She died in Jun 1969 in San Antonio, Texas.

23.   ii. VERA IONE NEATHERY was born on 23 Mar 1888 in Farmersville, Texas. She died on 15 Apr 1964 in Collin Coiunty, Texas. She married William Frederick Lampe on 17 Aug 1924. He was born on 27 Jul 1884 in Arlington, Texas. He died in Sep 1959 in Amarillo, Texas.

24.   iii. FAY EDWINA NEATHERY was born on 05 Dec 1889 in Farmersville, Texas. She died on 06 Apr 1971 in Los Angeles, California. She married Wallace B. Alexander, son of Franklin Gates Alexander and Mary Melvina Henry on 15 Dec 1908 in Haskell County, Texas. He was born on 29 Oct 1888 in Haskell, Texas. He died in Dec 1964 in Ruidosa, New Mexico.

25.   iv. DERON ADELLE NEATHERY was born on 06 Apr 1892 in Farmersville, Texas. She died on 13 Aug 1972. She married John Richard Oates on 12 Apr 1911 in Haskell, Texas. He was born in Jan 1891 in Livingston, Texas. He died on 03 Dec 1965 in Tarrant County, Texas.

26.   v.   SHIRLEY LORENE NEATHERY was born on 10 Mar 1893 in Farmersville, Texas. She died on 02 Jun 1980 in Fort Worth, Texas. She married Alexander Bruce Withers on 17 Aug 1914 in Dallas, Texas. He was born on 10 Aug 1891 in Mineral Wells, Texas.

        vi.   EDWARD ALLEN NEATHERY was born on 23 Feb 1900 in Farmersville, Texas. He died on 23 Sep 1971 in Dallas County, Texas. He married CLARINE WATSON. She was born on 03 Feb 1904. She died on 12 Jan 1975 in Dallas, Texas.
              Notes for Edward Allen Neathery:
              Had no children.

27.   vii. BARNEY LEE NEATHERY was born on 24 Dec 1901 in Farmersville, Texas. He died on 12 Jul 1973 in Seymour, Texas. He married Gladys Edith England on 17 Mar 1927. She was born on 07 Apr 1903 in Commerce, Texas.

28.   viii. ELSA LUCILLE NEATHERY was born on 11 Apr 1904 in Farmersville, Texas. She died in Sep 1992. She married (1) WILLIAM RICHARD WEINERT in Haskell, Texas. He was born on 22 Mar 1900 in Sequin, Texas. He died on 03 May 1944 in San Antonio, Texas. She married RUFUS W. MAJORS. He was born on 17 Jul 1895. He died on 07 Jun 1968.

5.   **WILLIE MAUD[2] EDWARDS** (William Archibald[1]) was born on 22 Aug 1868 in Autauga County, Alabama. She died on 04 Aug 1946 in Dallas, Texas. She married Thomas Benton Lester on 03 Dec 1886 in Caddo, Indian Territory (Oklahoma). He was born on 29 Feb 1856 in Mississippi. He died on 13 Apr 1928 in Dallas, Texas.

More About Willie Maud Edwards:
Burial: 05 Aug 1946 in Oak Cliff Cemetery, Dallas, Texas
Cause Of Death: Carcinoma of Breast
Occupation: 1910 in Dallas County, Texas; Working at dairy with her husband
Occupation: 1920 in Dallas, Dallas County, Texas; Seamstress
Occupation: 1930 in Dallas, Dallas County, Texas; Proprietor of Retail Grocery

More About Thomas Benton Lester:
Burial: 14 Apr 1928 in Oak Cliff Cemetery, Dallas, Texas
Cause Of Death: Bronchial Pneumonia
Occupation: 1880 in Denton County, Texas; Farm Laborer
Occupation: 1900 in Dallas County, Texas; Manager
Occupation: 1910 in Dallas County, Texas; Dairy Manager
Occupation: 1920 in Dallas, Dallas County, Texas; None
Occupation: Merchant

Thomas Benton Lester and Willie Maud Edwards had the following children:
        i.   EULA AGNES[3] LESTER was born on 24 Aug 1887. She died on 19 Oct 1887.

        ii.   MARY LEE LESTER was born on 19 Aug 1888 in Old Alton, Texas. She died in Jan 1891.

        iii. WILLIE ELIZA LESTER was born on 25 Sep 1890 in Denton, Texas. She died in 1983. She married C. B. Smith on 24 Sep 1911.

    iv.   LOIS LESTER was born on 16 Aug 1892 in Lewisville, Texas. She died in Jul 1894.

    v.   MAUDE LESTER was born on 08 Feb 1894 in Old Alton, Texas. She died on 28 Jan 1969. She married John Murrell in 1912.

More About Maude Lester:
Burial: Oak Cliff Cemetery, Dallas, Texas

    vi.   BRYAN LEWIS LESTER was born on 04 Apr 1896 in Dallas County, Texas. He died on 10 Jul 1952. He married Eula Morris on 17 Sep 1914.

    vii.   WILLIAM ARCHIBALD EDWARDS LESTER was born on 31 Jul 1898 in Dallas County, Texas. He married Rose Brennon in Jan 1921.

More About William Archibald Edwards Lester:
Occupation: 1920 in Dallas, Dallas County, Texas; Switchboard Operator at Telephone Company.

29.   viii.   DOROTHY LESTER was born on 14 Feb 1900 in Dallas County, Texas. She died on 16 Jun 1924 in Dallas, Texas. She married Charles Clarence Carter in Nov 1918. He was born on 11 Apr 1900 in Terrell, Texas. He died on 04 Jun 1972 in Oregon.

    x.   GLADYS LESTER was born on 10 Mar 1902. She died on 16 Jan 1903.

30.   x.   TOMMIE LESTER was born on 11 Jul 1905 in Dallas County, Texas. She died on 16 Apr 1986 in Harris County, Texas. She married David McMinn Belt, son of David Belt and Alice Langston on 19 Oct 1924. He was born on 02 Jun 1899 in Waxahachie, Ellis County, Texas. He died on 05 May 1943 in Dallas, Dallas County, Texas.

6.   CARRIE LOUISE[2] EDWARDS (William Archibald[1]) was born on 30 Sep 1871 in Autaugaville, Alabama. She died on 25 Nov 1971 in Albuquerque, New Mexico. She married James Lee Wilson, son of William Henry Wilson and Elizabeth C. Pickens on 27 Feb 1889 in Mt. Pleasant, Texas. He was born on 09 Mar 1863 in Franklin, Holmes County, Mississippi. He died on 23 Jan 1917 in Celina, Collin County, Texas.

More About Carrie Louise Edwards:
Burial: 27 Nov 1971 in West Hill Cemetery, Grayson County, Texas
Occupation: 1920 in Celina, Collin County, Texas; Post Mistress
Occupation: 1930 in Wichita Falls, Texas; Teacher at Private School
Occupation: 1940 in Wichita Falls, Texas; None

More About James Lee Wilson:
Burial: West Hill Cemetery, Grayson County, Texas
Occupation: 1900 in Sherman, Texas; Editor
Occupation: 1910 in Collinsville, Texas; Newspaper Editor
Occupation: 1917 in Celina, Texas; Postmaster
Occupation: Newspaper Owner and Editor

Notes for James Lee Wilson:
Death certificate has March 6, 1863 for date of birth.

James Lee Wilson and Carrie Louise Edwards had the following children:

31.   i.   WILLIAM HENRY[3] WILSON was born on 13 Dec 1889 in McKinney, Texas. He died on 26 Apr 1959 in Dallas, Texas. He married EVELYN STORM. She was born in Quitman, Texas.

        iii.   DOROTHY WILSON.

32.   iii.   ARIZONA WILSON was born on 29 Aug 1891 in Phoenix, Arizona. She died on 07 Apr 1977 in Little Rock, Arkansas. She married John Wesley Jackson on 24 Aug 1924.

        iv.   BENJAMIN LEE JONES WILSON was born on 18 Jul 1893 in Sherman, Texas.

Notes for Benjamin Lee Jones Wilson: Died in infancy.

        v.   MATTILYN WILSON was born on 17 Aug 1898 in Sherman, Texas.

7.   MATTIE ELIZABETH[2] EDWARDS (William Archibald[1]) was born on 30 Sep 1871 in Autaugaville, Alabama. She died on 15 Oct 1969 in Dallas, Texas. She married Benjamin Lee Jones, son of William Edwards Jones and Lonette Holcombe on 27 Feb 1889 in Mt. Pleasant, Texas. He was born on 18 Mar 1862 in Collinsville, Texas. He died on 17 Sep 1937 in Dallas, Texas.

More About Mattie Elizabeth Edwards: Burial: Hillcrest Memorial Park, Dallas, Texas Cause Of Death: ; Cerebral Thrombosis

More About Benjamin Lee Jones:
Burial: Hillcrest Memorial Park, Dallas, Texas
Cause Of Death: Occlusion Of Coronary Artery
Occupation: 1895; Admitted to the Texas Bar.
Occupation: 1900 in Sherman, Texas; Lawyer
Occupation: Bet. Jan 1904-Jan 1912; District judge of the 15th Judicial District.
Occupation: 1910 in Sherman, Texas; Lawyer
Occupation: 1920 in Sherman, Texas; Lawyer
Occupation: 1930 in Dallas, Dallas County, Texas; Lawyer andJudge of Appeals Court
Occupation: 1937 in Dallas, Dallas County, Texas; Chief Justice of Court of Criminal Appeals

Benjamin Lee Jones and Mattie Elizabeth Edwards had the following children:

33.   i.   CARRIE WINIFRED[3] JONES was born on 15 Nov 1889 in Van Alstyne, Texas. She died on 08 Sep 1977. She married Clarence Hugh McDaniel, son of E. M. McDaniel and Sophia Fulton on 16 Oct 1920 in Sherman, Texas. He was born on 29 Oct 1892 in Birmingham, Alabama. He died on 07 Apr 1970.

        ii.   CHARLES EDWARDS JONES was born on 28 Jan 1891 in Dallas, Texas. He died on 2 Feb 1891.

        iii.   LAURA GLADYS JONES was born on 16 Jan 1893 in Dallas, Texas. She died on 24 May 1894.

34.   iv.   JAMES WILLIAM JONES was born on 05 Oct 1894 in Whitesboro, Texas. He died on 3 Feb 1981 in Dallas, Texas. He married Charlotte Ellen LeMay on 21 Apr 1915 in Dallas, Texas. She was born on 12 Jan 1895 in Mahtowa,Minnesota.

     v.   BENJAMIN LEE JONES was born on 01 Oct 1900 in Sherman, Texas.

35.   vi.   MARJORY RUTH JONES was born on 13 Apr 1904 in Sherman, Texas. She died on 18 Oct 1998 in Brown County, Texas. She married CHARLES CRAIG WOODSON. He was born on 06 Aug 1898 in Searcy, Arkansas. He died on 23 May 1971.

36.   vii. ROBERT WINTON JONES was born on 14 Jul 1906 in Sherman, Texas. He married LILLIAN AMELIA HANEY. She was born on 19 Jul 1904 in Dallas, Texas.

8.   ELIZA EMELINE[2] EDWARDS (William Archibald[1]) was born on 09 Sep 1874 in Summerfield, Alabama. She died on 20 Jan 1964 in Dallas, Texas. She married George Henry Cochran, son of James Monroe Cochran and Margaret Lively on 30 Oct 1895 in Dallas, Texas. He was born on 04 Oct 1870 in Dallas, Texas. He died on 05 Apr 1956 in Dallas, Texas.

More About Eliza Emeline Edwards:
Burial: 22 Jan 1964 in Cochran Chapel Cemetery, Dallas,
Texas
Cause Of Death: Cerebral Thrombosis

More About George Henry Cochran:
Burial: 06 Apr 1956 in Cochran Chapel Cemetery, Dallas,
Texas Cause Of Death: Pneumonia
Occupation: 1900 in Dallas County, Texas; Farmer
Occupation: 1910 in Dallas County, Texas; Farmer
Occupation: 1920 in Dallas, Dallas County, Texas; Vice President of Skillern Drug Store Chain, Dallas, Texas
Occupation: 1930 in Dallas, Dallas County, Texas; Vice President of Skillern Drug Store Chain, Dallas, Texas

Notes for George Henry Cochran:
Headstone has October 4, 1870 for date of birth. Death certificate has October 2, 1870 for date of birth.

George Henry Cochran and Eliza Emeline Edwards had the following children:

     i.   MARGARET ELIZABETH[3] COCHRAN was born on 23 Nov 1901 in Dallas, Texas.

    More About Margaret Elizabeth Cochran:
    Living In: 1930 Living with her parents in Dallas, Texas.
    Occupation: 1930 in Dallas, Dallas County, Texas; Public School Teacer

     ii.   NELL COCHRAN was born about 1908.

    More About Nell Cochran:
    Living In: 1930 Living with her parents in Dallas, Texas.
    Occupation: 1930 in Dallas, Dallas County, Texas; Public School Teacher

Generation 3

9.   CLARA LILLIAN[3] EDWARDS (Theophilus Ambrose[2], William Archibald[1]) was born on 12 Feb 1884 in Farmersville, Texas. She died on 26 Oct 1973 in Ennis, Texas. She married Robert Roy Connally on 22 Sep 1904 in Waxahachie, Texas. He was born on 28 Sep 1881 in Ellis County, Texas.

More About Clara Lillian Edwards:
Burial: Hillcrest, Texas

Robert Roy Connally and Clara Lillian Edwards had the following children:

37. i. ROBERT EDWARDS[4] CONNALLY was born on 15 Jan 1906 in Waxahachie, Texas. He died on 18 Feb 1997 in Dallas County, Texas. He married (1) MARY LELA POWELL on 14 May 1929 in Houston, Texas. She was born on 18 Oct 1909. He married (2) ESTHER RUTH EASON on 09 Sep 1947. She was born on 11 May 1912.

38. ii. FRANK LEONARD CONNALLY was born on 13 Jun 1908 in Waxahachie, Texas. He married Catherine Snyder on 12 May 1929. She was born on 23 Oct 1911 in Bombarton, Texas.

39. iii. WALTER HORACE CONNALLY was born on 12 Jun 1912 in Waxahachie, Texas. He died on 12 Dec 1987 in Waxahachie, Texas. He married Mary Louise Braden on 18 Apr 1958. She was born on 12 Oct 1916.

40. iv. JAMES MARVIN CONNALLY was born on 09 Nov 1916 in Waxahachie, Texas. He married Tommie Eason on 15 Aug 1953.

10. **LAURA LEE OLIA[3] EDWARDS** (Theophilus Ambrose[2], William Archibald[1]) was born on 09 Aug 1886 in Nevada, Texas. She died on 31 May 1981. She married Robert Weldford Troth on 17 Oct 1911 in Dallas, Texas. He was born on 20 Mar 1880 in Zachary, Louisiana. He died on 02 Feb 1951.

Robert Weldford Troth and Laura Lee Olia Edwards had the following children:

41. i. NORA ELIZABETH[4] TROTH was born on 23 May 1912 in Dallas, Texas. She married Ralph Colvin Rodgers on 13 Apr 1939 in Dallas, Texas. He was born on 09 Jul 1906 in Cleburne, Texas.

42. ii. ROBERT WELDFORD TROTH was born on 13 Dec 1916 in Dallas, Texas. He married Ruth Elma Connerly on 16 Aug 1947 in Dallas, Texas. She was born on 11 Feb 1923 in Dallas, Texas.

43. iii. ROSEMARY TROTH was born on 10 Oct 1920 in Dallas, Texas. She married William John Mullane on 13 Apr 1945. He was born on 07 Oct 1919 in Brooklyn, New York, New York.

44. iv. BARBARA RUTH TROTH was born on 25 Feb 1927 in Dallas, Texas. She married Richard Walter Davenport on 26 Dec 1948 in Dallas, Texas. He was born on 21 Jan 1926 in Dallas, Texas. He died on 24 Feb 1971.

11. **THEOPHILUS MARVIN[3] EDWARDS** (Theophilus Ambrose[2], William Archibald[1]) was born on 05 Sep 1888 in Farmersville, Texas. He died on 13 May 1969 in Dallas, Texas. He married Georgia Mae Barksdale on 12 Sep 1911 in Waxahachie, Texas. She was born on 27 Apr 1889 in Beckville, Texas. She died on 13 Apr 1986 in Dallas, Texas.

More About Theophilus Marvin Edwards:
Burial: 15 May 1969 in Restland Memorial Park, Dallas, Texas
Cause Of Death: Cerebral Thrombosis
Living In: 1942 Bryson, Texas
Occupation: Realty Investor

More About Theophilus Marvin Edwards and Georgia Mae Barksdale: Marriage License: 12 Sep 1911 in Ellis County, Texas

Marriage Fact: Married by W. M. Nevins

Theophilus Marvin Edwards and Georgia Mae Barksdale had the following children:

45.   i. THEOPHILUS MARVIN[4] EDWARDS was born on 10 Jan 1913 in Waxahachie, Ellis County, Texas. He died on 30 Apr 2008 in Dallas, Texas. He married Susan Kathleen Romberger on 21 Oct 1951 in Denton, Texas. She was born on 12 Jan 1928.

46.   ii. FRANCES JANE EDWARDS was born on 10 Feb 1915 in Waxahachie, Texas. She died on 14 May 1984 in Nashville, Tennessee. She married Evans Moore Clements on 15 Jun 1940 in Nashville, Tennessee. He was born on 01 Apr 1915.

47.   iii. KATHERINE ANN EDWARDS was born on 13 Sep 1918 in Dallas, Dallas County, Texas. She married Roy Thorne Durst on 19 Feb 1938 in Dallas, Texas. He was born on 15 Nov 1914 in Mason, Texas. He died in 1999.

           iv. WILLIAM PRESLEY EDWARDS was born on 29 Nov 1922 in Dallas, Dallas County, Texas. He died on 29 Jan 1933 in Longview, Texas.

           More About William Presley Edwards:
           Burial: Restland Memorial Park, Dallas, Texas

12.   **RUBY ELIZABETH[3] EDWARDS** (Theophilus Ambrose[2], William Archibald[1]) was born on 15 Nov 1893 in Waxahachie, Texas. She died on 24 Sep 1966 in Dallas, Texas. She married Luther Price Robertson on 06 Oct 1924 in Arlington, Texas. He was born on 10 Oct 1893. He died on 25 Dec 1971.

Luther Price Robertson and Ruby Elizabeth Edwards had the following children:

48.   i. BETTY RUTH[4] ROBERTSON was born on 04 Aug 1925 in Dallas, Texas. She married Orien Neil Justice on 25 Mar 1944 in Dallas, Texas. He was born on 01 May 1923.

49.   ii. MARGY LEE ROBERTSON was born on 05 May 1928 in Dallas, Texas. She married (1) GEORGE WASHINGTON DAVIS on 29 Apr 1945 in Dallas, Texas. He was born on 22 Jan 1921. She married (2) THOMAS JEFFERSON WATSON on 12 Dec 1959 in Dallas, Texas. He was born on 22 Dec 1927. He died on 23 Aug 1974. She married (3) MARVIN WILSON on 16 Nov 1975. He was born on 29 May 1926.

13.   **WILLIAM ARTHUR[3] SKILLERN** (Mary James Cora[2] Edwards, William Archibald[1] Edwards) was born on 05 Aug 1885 in Lewisville, Texas. He died on 10 Jan 1922 in Dallas, Texas. He married Verna Lee Malone on 18 Jun 1907 in Dallas, Texas. She died on 20 Jul 1980.

      More About William Arthur Skillern:
      Burial: 11 Jan 1922 in Oak Cliff Cemetery, Dallas, Texas
      Occupation: Druggist

William Arthur Skillern and Verna Lee Malone had the following child:

50.   i. EDNA MADGE[4] SKILLERN. She died on 18 Oct 1970 in Dallas County, Texas. She married JOHN BAILEY PEYTON. He was born on 03 Apr 1906. He died in Jan 1983 in Dallas County, Texas.

14.   **FRANK LLOYD[3] SKILLERN** (Mary James Cora[2] Edwards, William Archibald[1] Edwards) was born on 5 Aug 1886 in Lewisville, Texas. He died on 26 Jan 1917 in Dallas, Texas. He married Elizabeth Peyton on 01 Oct 1908. She was born about 1889 in Texas.

More About Frank Lloyd Skillern:
Burial: 28 Jan 1917 in Oak Cliff Cemetery, Dallas, Texas
Occupation: 1910; Merchant, Dallas, Texas
Occupation: Druggist

Notes for Frank Lloyd Skillern:
Death Certificate gives August 24,1886 as date of Birth.

Frank Lloyd Skillern and Elizabeth Peyton had the following child:

51.   i. FRANK LLOYD[4] SKILLERN was born in 1915. He died on 24 Jan 1983 in Dallas County, Texas. He married MARTHA BARBARA ALLEN. She was born on 13 Jan 1913 in Hollister, California. She died on 03 Aug 1975 in Dallas, Texas.

15.   EDNA CORA[3] SKILLERN (Mary James Cora[2] Edwards, William Archibald[1] Edwards) was born on 31 Oct 1887 in Lewisville, Texas. She died on 21 Dec 1962 in Dallas, Texas. She married William Frank Cofer, son of Peter Joseph Cofer and Paulina Sawyer on 16 Apr 1912 in Dallas, Texas. He was born on 10 Mar 1884 in Illinois. He died on 13 Dec 1964 in Dallas, Dallas County, Texas.

More About Edna Cora Skillern:
Burial: 22 Dec 1962 in Laurel Land Cemetery, Dallas, Texas

More About William Frank Cofer:
Burial: 15 Dec 1964 in Laurel Land Cemetery, Dallas, Texas
Occupation: Drug Company Vice President

William Frank Cofer and Edna Cora Skillern had the following children:

52.   i. MARY ANN[4] COFER was born on 21 Jun 1917. She married Edward Preston Sneed on 10 May 1941. He was born on 19 Jul 1914. He died on 19 Mar 1995 in Dallas, Texas.

         ii. MARJORIE COFER was born in 1919. She married RALPH MILTON DUVAL.

53.   iii. WILLIAM FRANK COFER was born on 10 Mar 1923. He married DOROTHY NELL REESE. She was born on 31 Jul 1921.

         iv. ARTHUR JOSEPH COFER was born on 12 Sep 1925. He married MARY PORTER.

16.   LIDA[3] SKILLERN (Mary James Cora[2] Edwards, William Archibald[1] Edwards) was born on 15 Aug 1889 in Lewisville, Texas. She died on 29 Aug 1971 in Dallas, Texas. She married (1) **CHARLES BASCOM PETERSON** on 11 Apr 1911 in Dallas, Texas. She married **C. K. CONE**.

More About Lida Skillern:
Burial: 30 Aug 1971 in Oak Cliff Cemetery, Dallas, Texas
Cause Of Death: Acute and Progressive CVA

Charles Bascom Peterson and Lida Skillern had the following children:

         i CHARLES BASCOM[4] PETERSON.

54.   ii. MARY SUE PETERSON was born on 18 Jun 1927 in Dallas County, Texas. She married James Edgar Pope in Dallas, Texas.

17.   **RAE EDWARDS[3] SKILLERN** (Mary James Cora[2] Edwards, William Archibald[1] Edwards) was born on 01 Nov 1894 in Sherman, Texas. He died on 15 Aug 1964 in Denton, Texas. He married Anne Wilson on 19 Nov 1913 in Dallas, Texas. She was born in 1894. She died on 15 Aug 1964.

More About Rae Edwards Skillern:
Burial: 15 Aug 1964 in Hillcrest Mausoleum, Dallas, Texas
Cause Of Death: Fractured Skull from Automobile-Truck Accident
Occupation: President of Skillern and Son.

Rae Edwards Skillern and Anne Wilson had the following children:

55.   i. **BETTY EDWARDS[4] SKILLERN** was born on 23 Dec 1916. She died in 1999. She married Sam Aurelius Leake on 01 Jul 1938. He was born on 01 Dec 1914. He died in Jan 1996 in Dallas, Texas.

56.   ii. **ANNE RAE SKILLERN** was born on 31 Jul 1920. She married Andreas Franz Korn on 12 Jun 1947.

57.   iii. **JEAN REID SKILLERN** was born on 24 Dec 1928. She married Henry Wallace Meador on 15 Sep 1951.

18.   **ZULA[3] SKILLERN** (Mary James Cora[2] Edwards, William Archibald[1] Edwards) was born on 27 Aug 1899 in Dallas, Texas. She died on 16 Sep 1983 in Dallas, Texas. She married John Vest Folsom, son of Samuel Christopher Folsom and Agnes Ann Traller on 11 Mar 1920 in Dallas, Texas. He was born on 11 Nov 1898 in Coryell County, Texas. He died on 18 Nov 1976.

Notes for Zula Skillern:
Zula Skillern And John Vest Folsom

John Vest Folsom was born in Coryell County on November 11, 1898 to Agnes Ann Traller and Samuel Christopher Folsom. Samuel, the son of Nancy Cobb and Elias Folsom, was born in Georgia in 1857. Agnes, the daughter of Sara Stevenson and Joseph H. Traller, was born in Gatesville on July 5, 1869. Her father was born at sea on November 16, 1832 to German emigrants en route to America. Her mother was born on August 19, 1842 in Arkansas to Emily Jane and James Hall Stevenson.

Zula Skillern was born in Dallas County on August 29, 1899 to Mamie Jane Edwards and James Arthur Skillern. Mamie was born in Dale County, Alabama on September 6, 1864 to Elizabeth Jane White and William A. Edwards, both natives of Georgia. James was born in Bledsoe County, Tennessee on May 29, 1856 to Sarah and William Skillern. His earliest ancestor in America was William Skillern, born in Ireland about 1710. Mamie and James were married in 1884 in Denton County. He died in 1914 and she in 1935, and both are buried in the Oak Cliff Cemetery in Dallas.

Zula's father, James Skillern, was in Lewisville by 1880, where he established a drug store in 1885. By 1910 the company was known as Skillern and Sons Drugs and had numerous stores throughout north Texas, with headquarters in Dallas. Her grandfather, William A. Edwards, was a prominent Methodist minister and a captain in the Confederate army. Between 1886 and 1900 Reverend Edwards served as pastor of many north Texas churches, including Cochran Chapel, East Dallas, West Dallas, and Haskell Avenue Methodist.

Samuel Folsom, father of John Vest, was a prominent farmer in Coryell County, who died in 1920 and is buried in the Mount Cemetery in Coryell County.

During World War I, J.V. was stationed with the army at Love Field and he remained in Dallas the rest of his life. On March 20, 1920 he and Zula were married. Zula had graduated from Oak Cliff

High School and attended SMU and was active in a number of charitable, social, and women's organizations in Dallas. Both Zula and J.V. were very active in the Oak Cliff Methodist Church and J.V. served as a leader of the North Texas Conference of the United Methodist Church and also as president of the Methodist Hospital Board.

J.V. worked with his brothers in Dallas during the 1920s and thirties at the Folsom Company, manufacturing attic fans and space heaters. The company also represented small national manufacturers as sales representatives in the southwest. In 1940 the organization was divided into two separate companies: brother Al took the manufacturing business and J.V. took the sales representative business. J.V. founded the J.V. Folsom Company, a manufacturer's representative company for house wares and garden equipment.

J.V. died on November 18, 1976 and Zula died on September 16, 1983. Both are entombed in the Hillcrest Mausoleum.

J.V. and Zula had two sons, John, Jr. and Robert Skillern. J.V., Jr. was born on July 20, 1924 and attended SMU. He was a pilot in the U.S. Army Air Corps and died in December 1944 while serving in the Pacific area during World War II.

Robert Skillern was born in Dallas on February 15, 1927. He graduated from Sunset High School and attended the U.S. Military Academy at West Point near the end of World War II. He graduated in 1949 from SMU with a Bachelor of Business Administration degree and was a member of Kappa Alpha Order. Active in athletics, he lettered in football, basketball, baseball, and track.

Bob worked as a sales representative for the J.V. Folsom Company, but soon began real estate activity part time. By 1954 real estate was a full-time job. He became a major developer of shopping centers, office buildings, apartments, individual areas, and residential subdivisions. His interest in golf led him to build Bent Tree and Gleneagles Country Clubs.

Bob Folsom served on the boards of many civic and charitable organizations, including the Cotton Bowl Association, the D/FW Airport, Methodist Hospital, and SMU. He was mayor of the City of Dallas from 1976 to 1981 and president of the Dallas Independent School District Board from 1964 to 1966. He was president of many organizations including Preston Trail Golf Club 1985, 1993-1994; Dallas Country Club, 1966; Texas Municipal League 1979-1980; and SMU Alumni Association 1971-1972.

He has received numerous awards for business and civic activities, including SMU Distinguished Alumnus in 1975, Headliner of the Year Dallas Press Club award in 1981, J. Eric Jonsson Aviation Award in 1990, SMU Lettermen's Association Silver Anniversary Mustang Award in 1991, SMU Edwin Cox School of Business Distinguished Alumnus Award in 1995, and Award for Excellence in Humanities from the Dallas Historical Society in 2000.

Robert married Margaret Monet Dalton on March 7, 1949 and they have four children. Margaret Diane was born May 14, 1950 and married first Wayne Miller and second Robert Frank. Debbie was born November 9, 1953 and married Don Michael Jarma. John Vest, III was born May 1, 1956 and died May 30, 1983. Robert Stephen was born January 2, 1959 and married Sharon Marie St. Germaine.

By Steve Folsom

More About John Vest Folsom:
Military Service: U.S. Army, World War One.

John Vest Folsom and Zula Skillern had the following children:

      i. JOHN V .[4] FOLSOM was born on 20 Jul 1924 in Dallas, Texas. He died in Dec 1944 in Pacific Theater, World War Two.

More About John V. Folsom:
Military Service: Pilot, U.S. Army Air Force, World War Two

58. ii. ROBERT SKILLERN FOLSOM was born on 15 Feb 1927 in Dallas County, Texas. He married Margaret Monnette Dalton on 07 Mar 1949 in Dallas, Texas.

19. ZOLA[3] SKILLERN (Mary James Cora[2] Edwards, William Archibald[1] Edwards) was born on 27 Aug 1899 in Dallas, Texas. She died on 01 Sep 1951 in Dallas, Texas. She married (1) **WYLIE FONDREN WEATHERFORD**, son of William Eugene Weatherford and Alta Mary Gable on 29 Jul 1922 in Ferris, Texas. He was born on 20 Dec 1894 in Texas. He died on 31 Mar 1951 in Tarrant County, Texas. She married (2) **THOMAS CHAPMAN FERGUSON** in Aug 1941. He was born on 18 Jul 1908 in Pennsylvania. He died on 16 Apr 1983 in Tarrant County, Texas.

More About Zola Skillern:
Burial: 03 Sep 1951 in Hillcrest Mausoleum, Dallas, Texas
Cause Of Death: Liver Failure, Pneumonia and Cancer

More About Wylie Fondren Weatherford:
Burial: 01 Apr 1951 in Ferris Memorial Park North, Ferris, Ellis County, Texas
Military Service: U. S. Army, World War One

Wylie Fondren Weatherford and Zola Skillern had the following child:
59. i. WILLIAM EUGENE[4] WEATHERFORD was born on 02 Jul 1928. He died on 20 Sep 1998 in Dallas County, Texas. He married JUDITH WALLACE POLLARD. He married KAY HUGHES.

More About Thomas Chapman Ferguson:
Military Service: 11 Oct 1942 in Dallas, Texas; Enlisted in U.S. Army Air Force

20. **MARY EVELYN**[3] SKILLERN (Mary James Cora[2] Edwards, William Archibald[1] Edwards) was born on 15 Aug 1902 in Dallas, Texas. She died in Mar 1985 in Dallas, Texas. She married Leroy Monroe Napier, son of Leroy Munroe Napier on 10 Dec 1929. He was born on 19 Mar 1903. He died on 11 Jan 1969 in Dallas, Texas.

Leroy Monroe Napier and Mary Evelyn Skillern had the following children:
60. i. LEROY MONROE[4] NAPIER was born on 18 Jun 1935 in Dallas County, Texas. He married WILMA LEE FRANKLIN. He married BETTY PEARL BRADLEY.

  ii. JAMES SKILLERN NAPIER was born on 08 Jul 1940 in Dallas County, Texas. He married BETTY PEARL BRADLEY.

21. **JEAN**[3] SKILLERN (Mary James Cora[2] Edwards, William Archibald[1] Edwards) was born on 06 Dec 1906 in Dallas, Texas. She died on 17 Dec 1969. She married Robert Donald Hancock in 1932.

Robert Donald Hancock and Jean Skillern had the following children:
  i. GERRY[4] HANCOCK was born on 22 Feb 1937 in Dallas County, Texas. She married ROBERT M. UNSELL.

62. ii. ROBERT DONALD HANCOCK was born on 31 Jan 1940 in Dallas County, Texas. He married KAREN SUE DUGGAN.

22. **ORPHIE WILBUR**[3] **NEATHERY** (Annie Lee[2] Edwards, William Archibald[1] Edwards) was born on 17 Oct 1885 in Farmersville, Texas. He died on 03 May 1953 in Mangum, Oklahoma. He married Connie Wills in Apr 1909 in Wichita Falls, Texas. She was born on 26 Feb 1887. She died in Jun 1969 in San Antonio, Texas.

Orphie Wilbur Neathery and Connie Wills had the following child:

62.   i. ORPHIE[4] NEATHERY was born on 26 Apr 1912 in Haskell, Texas. He died on 15 Sep 1978. He married THELMA WINCHESTER. She was born on 01 May 1915. She died in Apr 1965.

23. **VERA IONE**[3] **NEATHERY** (Annie Lee[2] Edwards, William Archibald[1] Edwards) was born on 23 Mar 1888 in Farmersville, Texas. She died on 15 Apr 1964 in Collin Coiunty, Texas. She married William Frederick Lampe on 17 Aug 1924. He was born on 27 Jul 1884 in Arlington, Texas. He died in Sep 1959 in Amarillo, Texas.

William Frederick Lampe and Vera Ione Neathery had the following children:

63.   i. WILLIAM NEATHERY[4] LAMPE was born on 24 Jul 1926 in Amarillo, Texas. He married JIMMA JOANN DRAKE. She was born on 25 May 1929 in Hamlin, Texas.

64.   ii. ALMA RUTH LAMPE was born on 07 Apr 1929 in Amarillo, Texas. She married JAMES RAY MCKENZIE. He was born on 14 Feb 1925 in Van, Texas.

24. **FAY EDWINA**[3] **NEATHERY** (Annie Lee[2] Edwards, William Archibald[1] Edwards) was born on 05 Dec 1889 in Farmersville, Texas. She died on 06 Apr 1971 in Los Angeles, California. She married Wallace B. Alexander, son of Franklin Gates Alexander and Mary Melvina Henry on 15 Dec 1908 in Haskell County, Texas. He was born on 29 Oct 1888 in Haskell, Texas. He died in Dec 1964 in Ruidosa, New Mexico.

Wallace B. Alexander and Fay Edwina Neathery had the following children:

65.   i. MARY ANN[4] ALEXANDER was born on 22 Sep 1912 in Haskell, Texas. She married Eldon Luther Hill in Dec 1942 in Seymour, Texas.

66.   ii. EVELYN FAYE ALEXANDER was born on 15 Oct 1915 in Haskell, Texas. She died on 18 Mar 1984 in Quitman, Texas. She married Roy Stanley Lankford, son of Montiville Lankford and Roxanna Gorman on 03 Feb 1935 in Frederick, Oklahoma. He was born on 29 Jan 1909 in Seymour, Texas. He died on 21 May 1992 in Longview, Texas.

67.   iii. RUTH ALEXANDER was born on 14 Sep 1918 in Palestine, Texas. She married Thomas Woodard Smith on 17 Jan 1942 in Seymour, Texas. He was born on 13 Jul 1917 in Center, Texas. He died on 02 Oct 1980 in Austin, Texas.

68.   iv. CONSTANCE ALEXANDER was born on 07 Jul 1923 in Seymour, Texas. She married (1) HARRY TAULMAN BOWERS on 09 Dec 1941 in Fort Worth, Texas. She married (2) FREDERICK P. STOCKMAN on 24 May 1977 in Los Angeles, California.

25. **DERON ADELLE**[3] **NEATHERY** (Annie Lee[2] Edwards, William Archibald[1] Edwards) was born on 06 Apr 1892 in Farmersville, Texas. She died on 13 Aug 1972. She married John Richard Oates on 12 Apr 1911 in Haskell, Texas. He was born in Jan 1891 in Livingston, Texas. He died on 03 Dec 1965 in Tarrant County, Texas.

John Richard Oates and Deron Adelle Neathery had the following child:

69.   i. JOHN RICHARD[4] OATES was born on 17 May 1914 in Haskell, Texas. He died on 27 Dec 1980 in Bell County, Texas. He married (1) LONELLE WHITAKER on 24 Nov 1938. He married JEFFIE MAE TURPEN. She was born on 10 Mar 1914 in Redford,

Indiana.

26.   **SHIRLEY LORENE**[3] **NEATHERY** (Annie Lee[2] Edwards, William Archibald[1] Edwards) was born on 10 Mar 1893 in Farmersville, Texas. She died on 02 Jun 1980 in Fort Worth, Texas. She married Alexander Bruce Withers on 17 Aug 1914 in Dallas, Texas. He was born on 10 Aug 1891 in Mineral Wells, Texas.

More About Shirley Lorene Neathery:
Burial: Mineral Wells, Texas

Alexander Bruce Withers and Shirley Lorene Neathery had the following child:

70.   i.   JENNY LEE[4] WITHERS was born on 05 Dec 1915 in Dallas, Texas. She married AMBRIS VETETO.

27.   **BARNEY LEE**[3] **NEATHERY** (Annie Lee[2] Edwards, William Archibald[1] Edwards) was born on 24 Dec 1901 in Farmersville, Texas. He died on 12 Jul 1973 in Seymour, Texas. He married Gladys Edith England on 17 Mar 1927. She was born on 07 Apr 1903 in Commerce, Texas.

More About Barney Lee Neathery:
Occupation: 1920 in Haskell, Haskell County, Texas; Salesman at Drug Store

Barney Lee Neathery and Gladys Edith England had the following children:

71.   i.   NELDA LYNN[4] NEATHERY was born on 13 Feb 1932. She married Russell Larry Robinson on 29 Aug 1953. He died in 1968.

72.   ii.   GLADYS ANN NEATHERY was born on 14 Feb 1934. She married MAX KING.

28.   **ELSA LUCILLE**[3] **NEATHERY** (Annie Lee[2] Edwards, William Archibald[1] Edwards) was born on 11 Apr 1904 in Farmersville, Texas. She died in Sep 1992. She married (1) **WILLIAM RICHARD WEINERT** in Haskell, Texas. He was born on 22 Mar 1900 in Sequin, Texas. He died on 03 May 1944 in San Antonio, Texas. She married **RUFUS W. MAJORS**. He was born on 17 Jul 1895. He died on 07 Jun 1968.

More About William Richard Weinert:
Burial: 05 May 1944 in Haskell, Texas

William Richard Weinert and Elsa Lucille Neathery had the following children:

73.   i.   JEANETTE LUCILLE[4] WEINERT was born on 24 Sep 1922 in Haskell, Texas. She married GEORGE J. ROEBER. He was born on 22 Jan 1921.

74.   ii.   ANNIE LEE WEINERT was born on 26 Apr 1926 in Weinert, Texas. She married DONALD E. WEISE. He was born on 29 Mar 1922.

75.   iii.   WILLIAM RICHARD WEINERT was born on 18 Oct 1929 in Weinert, Texas. He married HAZEL CLAIRE TURNER.

29.   **DOROTHY**[3] **LESTER** (Willie Maud[2] Edwards, William Archibald[1] Edwards) was born on 14 Feb 1900 in Dallas County, Texas. She died on 16 Jun 1924 in Dallas, Texas. She married Charles Clarence Carter in Nov 1918. He was born on 11 Apr 1900 in Terrell, Texas. He died on 04 Jun 1972 in Oregon.

More About Dorothy Lester:

Burial: 17 Jun 1924 in Oak Cliff Cemetery, Dallas, Texas
Cause Of Death: Complications of Childbirth

More About Charles Clarence Carter:
Burial: Mulkey Cemetery, Eugene, Lane County, Oregon
Occupation: 1919 - Telephone Company Worker

Charles Clarence Carter and Dorothy Lester had the following children:

76. i. CHARLES CLARENCE[4] CARTER was born on 14 Jul 1919 in Dallas, Dallas County, Texas. He died on 17 Mar 2002 in Plano, Texas. He married NELLIS RHEA DIXON. She was born on 20 Oct 1921 in Dallas, Dallas County, Texas. She died on 30 Aug 2005 in Plano, Texas.

77. ii. DOROTHY JUANITA CARTER was born on 15 Nov 1920 in Dallas, Dallas County, Texas. She married PERRY IKE BLEVINS. He was born on 09 Jun 1914 in Holdenville, Huges County, Oklahoma. He died on 15 Apr 1996 in Fresno County, California.

 iii. INFANT CARTER was born on 22 Aug 1922 in Dallas, Dallas County, Texas. He died on 24 Aug 1922 in Dallas, Dallas County, Texas.

 iv. INFANT CARTER was born on 16 Jun 1924 in Dallas, Dallas County, Texas. He died on 16 Jun 1924 in Dallas, Dallas County, Texas.

30. TOMMIE[3] LESTER (Willie Maud[2] Edwards, William Archibald[1] Edwards) was born on 11 Jul 1905 in Dallas County, Texas. She died on 16 Apr 1986 in Harris County, Texas. She married David McMinn Belt, son of David Belt and Alice Langston on 19 Oct 1924. He was born on 02 Jun 1899 in Waxahachie, Ellis County, Texas. He died on 05 May 1943 in Dallas, Dallas County, Texas.

More About Tommie Lester:
Living In: 1930 Divorced and living with her mother in Dallas, Texas
Occupation: 1930 in Dallas, Dallas County, Texas; Stenographer

More About David McMinn Belt:
Burial: 07 May 1943 in Lisbon Cemetery, Dallas, Dallas County, Texas
Occupation: 1943 in Dallas, Texas; Aircraft Worker for North American Aviation
Inc. Military Service: Bet. 17 May-11 Dec 1918; U. S. Navy

David McMinn Belt and Tommie Lester had the following child:

 i. JAMES EDWARD[4] BELT was born on 19 Aug 1925 in Dallas, Dallas County, Texas. He married WYNONAH (UNKNOWN). She was born in 1925.

31. WILLIAM HENRY[3] WILSON (Carrie Louise[2] Edwards, William Archibald[1] Edwards) was born on 13 Dec 1889 in McKinney, Texas. He died on 26 Apr 1959 in Dallas, Texas. He married EVELYN STORM. She was born in Quitman, Texas.

More About William Henry Wilson:
Burial: Restland Memorial Park, Dallas, Texas
Occupation: 1910 in Collinsville, Texas; Newspaper
Printer
Occupation: Lawyer

William Henry Wilson and Evelyn Storm had the following children:

78. i. JOHN FRANKLIN[4] WILSON was born in Sherman, Texas. He married MARCELLENE ROBERTS SNORF. She was born in Chicago, Illinois.

    ii.   JAMES LEE WILSON.

    iii.   WILLIAM HENRY WILSON.

79.   iv. EVELYN STORM WILSON was born on 25 Nov 1915 in Sherman, Texas. She married WARREN EASTWOOD TRACY.

32.   **ARIZONA**^{3} **WILSON** (Carrie Louise^2 Edwards, William Archibald^1 Edwards) was born on 29 Aug 1891 in Phoenix, Arizona. She died on 07 Apr 1977 in Little Rock, Arkansas. She married John Wesley Jackson on 24 Aug 1924.

More About Arizona Wilson:
Burial: Fairview Memorial Park, Albuquerque, New Mexico

John Wesley Jackson and Arizona Wilson had the following children:
    i.   JOHN WESLEY^4 JACKSON.

    ii.   DOROTHY ELAINE JACKSON.

33.   **CARRIE WINIFRED**^{3} **JONES** (Mattie Elizabeth^2 Edwards, William Archibald^1 Edwards) was born on 15 Nov 1889 in Van Alstyne, Texas. She died on 08 Sep 1977. She married Clarence Hugh McDaniel, son of E. M. McDaniel and Sophia Fulton on 16 Oct 1920 in Sherman, Texas. He was born on 29 Oct 1892 in Birmingham, Alabama. He died on 07 Apr 1970.

More About Carrie Winifred
Jones: Burial: Brownwood, Texas
Occupation: 1910 in Sherman, Texas; School Teacher

More About Clarence Hugh
McDaniel:
Burial: Brownwood, Texas

Clarence Hugh McDaniel and Carrie Winifred Jones had the following children:
    i.   ELIZABETH LEE^4 MCDANIEL was born on 10 Sep 1921 in Sherman, Texas. She married Clyde F. Gafford on 13 May 1949 in Rockwall, Texas. He was born on 06 Jul 1911 in Burkett, Texas. He died on 17 Jun 1978 in Dallas, Texas.

81.   ii. JEAN RUTH MCDANIEL was born on 10 Feb 1924 in Handley, Texas. She married Harry Edward Ailey on 06 Jul 1942 in Dallas, Texas. He died on 11 Nov 1974.

34.   **JAMES WILLIAM**^{3} **JONES** (Mattie Elizabeth^2 Edwards, William Archibald^1 Edwards) was born on 05 Oct 1894 in Whitesboro, Texas. He died on 03 Feb 1981 in Dallas, Texas. He married Charlotte Ellen LeMay on 21 Apr 1915 in Dallas, Texas. She was born on 12 Jan 1895 in Mahtowa,Minnesota.

More About James William Jones:
Occupation: 1920 in Sherman, Texas; Military School Instructor

James William Jones and Charlotte Ellen LeMay had the following children:
    i.   PATRICIA CHARLOTTE^4 JONES was born about 1917 in Texas.

    ii.   MARTHA LEMAY JONES was born on 03 Nov 1919 in Sherman, Texas.

iii.   JAMES WILLIAM JONES.

35.   **MARJORY RUTH**[3] **JONES** (Mattie Elizabeth[2] Edwards, William Archibald[1] Edwards) was born on 13 Apr 1904 in Sherman, Texas. She died on 18 Oct 1998 in Brown County, Texas. She married **CHARLES CRAIG WOODSON**. He was born on 06 Aug 1898 in Searcy, Arkansas. He died on 23 May 1971.

More About Charles Craig Woodson:
Occupation: Newspaper Publisher

Charles Craig Woodson and Marjory Ruth Jones had the following children:

81.   i. CHARLES CRAIG[4] WOODSON was born on 22 Oct 1933 in Palestine, Texas. He married Peggy Loraine Mayfield on 20 Jun 1953 in Waco, Texas.

82.   ii. BEN JONES WOODSON was born on 24 Nov 1934 in Palestine, Texas. He married (1) DONI LOUISE RICHARDSON on 27 Dec 1955 in Lamesa, Texas. He married (2) SHIRLEY GREGORY BOYD on 02 Jan 1975.

83.   iii. JOHN ROSS WOODSON was born on 19 Mar 1938 in Dallas, Texas. He married Jo Alice Moglia in Dec 1969 in Austin, Texas.

36.   **ROBERT WINTON**[3] **JONES** (Mattie Elizabeth[2] Edwards, William Archibald[1] Edwards) was born on 14 Jul 1906 in Sherman, Texas. He married **LILLIAN AMELIA HANEY**. She was born on 19 Jul 1904 in Dallas, Texas.

More About Robert Winton Jones:
Occupation: 1930 in Dallas, Dallas County, Texas; General Accountant
Occupation: C.P.A. , Freeport Sulphur Company

Robert Winton Jones and Lillian Amelia Haney had the following children:

84.   i. CAROL ANN[4] JONES was born on 14 Sep 1930 in Dallas, Texas. She married Ira DuBois Johnson on 14 Aug 1954. He died about 1976.

ii.   JULIE JONES was born on 15 Nov 1943 in Dallas, Texas.

Generation 4

37.   **ROBERT EDWARDS**[4] **CONNALLY** (Clara Lillian[3] Edwards, Theophilus Ambrose[2] Edwards, William Archibald[1] Edwards) was born on 15 Jan 1906 in Waxahachie, Texas. He died on 18 Feb 1997 in Dallas County, Texas. He married (1) **MARY LELA POWELL** on 14 May 1929 in Houston, Texas. She was born on 18 Oct 1909. He married (2) **ESTHER RUTH EASON** on 09 Sep 1947. She was born on 11 May 1912.

Robert Edwards Connally and Mary Lela Powell had the following children:

85.   i. LELA PATRICIA[5] CONNALLY was born on 07 Mar 1930 in Houston, Texas. She married (1) EARL LEON WINGO on 23 Jul 1947 in Andalusia, Alabama. He was born on 03 Jul 1931 in Hattiesburg, Mississippi. She married (2) CLARK H. GILLILAND on 21 Jul 1971. She married DENNIS T. BARROW.

86.   ii. ROBERT EDWARDS CONNALLY was born on 16 Nov 1931 in Dallas, Texas. He died on 06 Feb 1979. He married Frances Bullock on 09 Aug 1955.

87.   iii.   LILLIAN CONNALLY was born on 19 Jul 1933 in Dallas, Texas. She married John

William Renfro on 16 Apr 1952.

88.   iv. MARY CONNALLY was born on 05 Nov 1936 in Montgomery, Alabama. She married Frank Garrett Daniel on 28 Dec 1955.

Robert Edwards Connally and Esther Ruth Eason had the following child:

v.   RUTH ELLEN C ONNALLY was born on 16 Feb 1948 in Galveston, Texas. She married WAYNE HAYS.

38.   **FRANK LEONARD**[4] **CONNALLY** (Clara Lillian[3] Edwards, Theophilus Ambrose[2] Edwards, William Archibald[1] Edwards) was born on 13 Jun 1908 in Waxahachie, Texas. He married Catherine Snyder on 12 May 1929. She was born on 23 Oct 1911 in Bombarton, Texas.

Frank Leonard Connally and Catherine Snyder had the following child:

89.   i. NANCY ANN[5] CONNALLY was born on 13 Dec 1931. She married Bill Joe Houck on 02 Feb 1951.

39.   **WALTER HORACE**[4] **CONNALLY** (Clara Lillian[3] Edwards, Theophilus Ambrose[2] Edwards, William Archibald[1] Edwards) was born on 12 Jun 1912 in Waxahachie, Texas. He died on 12 Dec 1987 in Waxahachie, Texas. He married Mary Louise Braden on 18 Apr 1958. She was born on 12 Oct 1916.

Notes for Mary Louise Braden:
Maiden name is listed in Texas birth index as Briles.

Walter Horace Connally and Mary Louise Braden had the following children:

i.   DOROTHY LOUISE[5] CONNALLY was born on 20 Feb 1959.

ii.   ROBERT JOE CONNALLY was born on 19 Feb 1960.

40.   **JAMES MARVIN**[4] **CONNALLY** (Clara Lillian[3] Edwards, Theophilus Ambrose[2] Edwards, William Archibald[1] Edwards) was born on 09 Nov 1916 in Waxahachie, Texas. He married Tommie Eason on 15 Aug 1953.

James Marvin Connally and Tommie Eason had the following children:

90.   i. CLARA ANN[5] CONNALLY was born on 10 Oct 1954. She married CHARLES WAYNE TOWNSON.

ii.   BARBARA JANE CONNALLY.

41.   **NORA ELIZABETH**[4] **TROTH** (Laura Lee Olia[3] Edwards, Theophilus Ambrose[2] Edwards, William Archibald[1] Edwards) was born on 23 May 1912 in Dallas, Texas. She married Ralph Colvin Rodgers on 13 Apr 1939 in Dallas, Texas. He was born on 09 Jul 1906 in Cleburne, Texas.

Ralph Colvin Rodgers and Nora Elizabeth Troth had the following children:

i.   ROBERT MARSHAL[5] RODGERS was born on 24 Jan 1943 in Dallas, Texas.

92.   ii. LEE OLIA RODGERS was born on 23 Oct 1945 in Dallas County, Texas. She married GLEN ARTHUR SALE.

42.   **ROBERT WELDFORD**[4] **TROTH** (Laura Lee Olia[3] Edwards, Theophilus Ambrose[2] Edwards, William Archibald[1] Edwards) was born on 13 Dec 1916 in Dallas, Texas. He married Ruth Elma Connerly on 16 Aug 1947 in Dallas, Texas. She was born on 11 Feb 1923 in Dallas, Texas.

Robert Weldford Troth and Ruth Elma Connerly had the following children:

92.   i. ANN ELIZABETH[5] TROTH was born on 03 Sep 1948 in Dallas County, Texas. She married Michael Mottern Coleman on 27 Jun 1969. He was born on 27 Dec 1946 in Pomona, California.

93.   ii. JANE FRANCES TROTH was born on 16 Nov 1950 in Dallas County, Texas. She married Richard Cummings McCorkle on 17 Jul 1971. He was born on 22 Mar 1950 in Dallas, Texas.

       iii. NANCY RUTH TROTH was born on 02 Aug 1952 in Dallas County, Texas.

       iv. PEGGY JEAN TROTH was born on 21 May 1954 in Dallas County, Texas.

43. **ROSEMARY[4] TROTH** (Laura Lee Olia[3] Edwards, Theophilus Ambrose[2] Edwards, William Archibald[1] Edwards) was born on 10 Oct 1920 in Dallas, Texas. She married William John Mullane on 13 Apr 1945. He was born on 07 Oct 1919 in Brooklyn, New York, New York.

William John Mullane and Rosemary Troth had the following children:

94.   i. LINDA ANN[5] MULLANE was born on 05 May 1948 in Dallas County, Texas. She married ROGER HUGHES KLINE. He was born on 16 May 1945 in Evanston, Illinois.

       ii. JOHN ROBERT MULLANE was born on 21 Apr 1955 in Dallas County, Texas.

44. **BARBARA RUTH[4] TROTH** (Laura Lee Olia[3] Edwards, Theophilus Ambrose[2] Edwards, William Archibald[1] Edwards) was born on 25 Feb 1927 in Dallas, Texas. She married Richard Walter Davenport on 26 Dec 1948 in Dallas, Texas. He was born on 21 Jan 1926 in Dallas, Texas. He died on 24 Feb 1971.

Richard Walter Davenport and Barbara Ruth Troth had the following children:

95.   i. SUSAN LEE[5] DAVENPORT was born on 15 Aug 1952 in Dallas County, Texas. She married Roy Michael Thomas on 14 Jun 1975. He was born on 15 Jul 1952 in Dallas, Texas.

       ii. ROSEMARY DAVENPORT was born on 16 Oct 1955 in Dallas County, Texas.

45. **THEOPHILUS MARVIN[4] EDWARDS** (Theophilus Marvin[3], Theophilus Ambrose[2], William Archibald[1]) was born on 10 Jan 1913 in Waxahachie, Ellis County, Texas. He died on 30 Apr 2008 in Dallas, Texas. He married Susan Kathleen Romberger on 21 Oct 1951 in Denton, Texas. She was born on 12 Jan 1928.

More About Theophilus Marvin Edwards:
Military Service: 24 May 1942; Enlisted in U.S. Army in Dallas, Texas

Theophilus Marvin Edwards and Susan Kathleen Romberger had the following children:

       i. WILLIAM MARVIN[5] EDWARDS was born on 29 Jun 1952 in Denton County, Texas. He died on 06 Jun 1976 in Dallas, Texas.

           More About William Marvin Edwards:
           Burial: 07 Jun 1976 in Restland Memorial Park, Dallas, Texas

96.   ii. GEORGE MARVIN EDWARDS was born on 16 Jun 1953 in Dallas County, Texas. He married Patti Susan Rush on 10 Mar 1979 in Dallas, Texas.

97. iii. CHARLES AUSTIN EDWARDS was born on 13 Jan 1955 in Dallas, Texas. He married ROMALDA ANN ALLSUP.

46. **FRANCES JANE**[4] **EDWARDS** (Theophilus Marvin[3], Theophilus Ambrose[2], William Archibald[1]) was born on 10 Feb 1915 in Waxahachie, Texas. She died on 14 May 1984 in Nashville, Tennessee. She married Evans Moore Clements on 15 Jun 1940 in Nashville, Tennessee. He was born on 01 Apr 1915.

Evans Moore Clements and Frances Jane Edwards had the following children:

98. i. EVANS MOORE[5] CLEMENTS was born on 21 May 1941 in Nashville, Tennessee. He married Harriet Vasti Greene on 19 Mar 1960 in Nashville, Tennessee. She was born on 21 Jan 1943.

99. ii. JANE EDWARDS CLEMENTS was born on 08 Oct 1942 in Nashville, Tennessee. She married David Wilson McMackin on 19 Jan 1963 in Nashville, Tennessee. He was born on 06 Dec 1937.

100. iii. MARVIN EDWARDS CLEMENTS was born on 21 Feb 1945 in Nashville, Tennessee. He married Patricia Martin on 20 Aug 1966. She was born on 18 Apr 1946.

47. **KATHERINE ANN**[4] **EDWARDS** (Theophilus Marvin[3], Theophilus Ambrose[2], William Archibald[1]) was born on 13 Sep 1918 in Dallas, Dallas County, Texas. She married Roy Thorne Durst on 19 Feb 1938 in Dallas, Texas. He was born on 15 Nov 1914 in Mason, Texas. He died in 1999.

Roy Thorne Durst and Katherine Ann Edwards had the following child:

101. i. BARBARA EDWARDS[5] DURST was born on 13 May 1942. She married Robert Hunter McLean on 22 Jun 1963. He was born on 26 Apr 1941.

48. **BETTY RUTH**[4] **ROBERTSON** (Ruby Elizabeth[3] Edwards, Theophilus Ambrose[2] Edwards, William Archibald[1] Edwards) was born on 04 Aug 1925 in Dallas, Texas. She married Orien Neil Justice on 25 Mar 1944 in Dallas, Texas. He was born on 01 May 1923.

Orien Neil Justice and Betty Ruth Robertson had the following children:

  i. TIMOTHY NEIL[5] JUSTICE was born on 01 Mar 1950 in Dallas, Texas. He married Patricia Day Jennings on 22 Jun 1978. She was born on 25 May 1953.

  ii. BETSY ROBIN JUSTICE was born on 30 Nov 1959 in Dallas, Texas.

49. **MARGY LEE**[4] **ROBERTSON** (Ruby Elizabeth[3] Edwards, Theophilus Ambrose[2] Edwards, William Archibald[1] Edwards) was born on 05 May 1928 in Dallas, Texas. She married (1) **GEORGE WASHINGTON DAVIS** on 29 Apr 1945 in Dallas, Texas. He was born on 22 Jan 1921. She married (2) **THOMAS JEFFERSON WATSON** on 12 Dec 1959 in Dallas, Texas. He was born on 22 Dec 1927. He died on 23 Aug 1974. She married (3) **MARVIN WILSON** on 16 Nov 1975. He was born on 29 May 1926.

George Washington Davis and Margy Lee Robertson had the following child:

102. i. CYNTHIA ELIZABETH[5] DAVIS was born on 01 Mar 1946 in Dallas County, Texas. She married Ronald L. Giles on 12 May 1965. He was born on 07 Apr 1943.

50. **EDNA MADGE**[4] **SKILLERN** (William Arthur[3], Mary James Cora[2] Edwards, William Archibald[1] Edwards, William Arthur[3], James Arthur, William Franklin). She died on 18 Oct 1970 in Dallas County, Texas. She married **JOHN BAILEY PEYTON**. He was born on 03 Apr 1906. He died in Jan 1983 in Dallas County, Texas.

Notes for John Bailey Peyton:
Nickname was "Jack".

John Bailey Peyton and Edna Madge Skillern had the following children:

    i.   JOHN BAILEY[5] PEYTON was born on 22 May 1942 in Dallas County, Texas. He married TINA GUERRIERO.

    ii.   PENELOPE SKILLERN PEYTON was born on 03 Dec 1947 in Dallas County, Texas. She married Don Erdman Coder on 02 Dec 1978 in Dallas County, Texas.

51.   **FRANK LLOYD[4] SKILLERN** (Frank Lloyd[3], Mary James Cora[2] Edwards, William Archibald[1] Edwards) was born in 1915. He died on 24 Jan 1983 in Dallas County, Texas. He married **MARTHA BARBARA ALLEN**. She was born on 13 Jan 1913 in Hollister, California. She died on 03 Aug 1975 in Dallas, Texas.

More About Martha Barbara Allen:
Burial: 05 Aug 1975 in Restland Memorial Park, Dallas, Texas

Frank Lloyd Skillern and Martha Barbara Allen had the following children:

    i.   FRANK LLOYD[5] SKILLERN was born on 10 Jul 1936 in Dallas County, Texas. He married Mary Eames Woolsey on 06 Apr 1968 in Dallas County, Texas.

104.   ii. CHRISTOPHER LEE SKILLERN was born on 30 Jun 1941 in Dallas County, Texas. He married SANDRA KISH.

105.   iii. ELIZABETH PEYTON SKILLERN was born on 30 Jan 1944 in Cameron County, Texas. She married ROBERT HAGERTY.

52.   **MARY ANN[4] COFER** (Edna Cora[3] Skillern, Mary James Cora[2] Edwards, William Archibald[1] Edwards) was born on 21 Jun 1917. She married Edward Preston Sneed on 10 May 1941. He was born on 19 Jul 1914. He died on 19 Mar 1995 in Dallas, Texas.

Edward Preston Sneed and Mary Ann Cofer had the following child:

105.   i. EDWARD PRESTON[5] SNEED was born on 01 Mar 1947 in Dallas County, Texas. He married BARBARA ALLEN HENRY.

53.   **WILLIAM FRANK[4] COFER** (Edna Cora[3] Skillern, Mary James Cora[2] Edwards, William Archibald[1] Edwards) was born on 10 Mar 1923. He married **DOROTHY NELL REESE**. She was born on 31 Jul 1921.

William Frank Cofer and Dorothy Nell Reese had the following children:

106.   i. CAROL JOY[5] COFER was born on 04 May 1950 in Dallas County, Texas. She married Loyd Frank Lewellen on 18 Mar 1967 in Dallas County, Texas.

107.   ii. JANET LEE COFER was born on 15 Dec 1951 in Dallas County, Texas. She married DAN THOMAS BOATRIGHT.

108.   iii. CYNTHIA ANN COFER was born on 22 Jul 1955 in Dallas County, Texas. She married MICHAEL LYNN WALL.

109.   iv. WILLIAM FRANK COFER was born on 09 Nov 1961 in Dallas County, Texas. He married CYNTHIA KAYE COLLINS.

54.   **MARY SUE[4] PETERSON** (Lida[3] Skillern, Mary James Cora[2] Edwards, William Archibald[1] Edwards)

was born on 18 Jun 1927 in Dallas County, Texas. She married James Edgar Pope in Dallas, Texas.

James Edgar Pope and Mary Sue Peterson had the following children:

110. i. JOHN CHARLES[5] POPE was born on 22 Feb 1951 in Dallas County, Texas. He married SHARON EVON SOLADAY. She was born on 28 Oct 1948 in Taylor County, Texas.

 ii. BARBARA POPE was born on 22 Feb 1955 in Dallas County, Texas.

55. **BETTY EDWARDS[4] SKILLERN** (Rae Edwards[3], Mary James Cora[2] Edwards, William Archibald[1] Edwards) was born on 23 Dec 1916. She died in 1999. She married Sam Aurelius Leake on 01 Jul 1938. He was born on 01 Dec 1914. He died in Jan 1996 in Dallas, Texas.

Sam Aurelius Leake and Betty Edwards Skillern had the following children:

111. i. SAM SKILLERN[5] LEAKE was born on 04 Oct 1941 in Dallas County, Texas. He married KATHARINE SEVERANCE SEARS.

 ii. DAVID HOBSON LEAKE was born on 13 Sep 1943 in Dallas County, Texas.

112. iii. JOHN WILSON LEAKE was born on 25 Dec 1948 in Dallas County, Texas. He married MARYANN WIGHAMAN.

56. **ANNE RAE[4] SKILLERN** (Rae Edwards[3], Mary James Cora[2] Edwards, William Archibald[1] Edwards) was born on 31 Jul 1920. She married Andreas Franz Korn on 12 Jun 1947.

Andreas Franz Korn and Anne Rae Skillern had the following children:

 i. ELIZABETH ANN[5] KORN was born on 24 May 1948 in Dallas County, Texas.

113. ii. RAE SKILLERN KORN was born on 01 Nov 1944 in Dallas County, Texas. He married DONNA LYNN SPEIGEL. He married BRENDA ANN MADDOX.

57. **JEAN REID[4] SKILLERN** (Rae Edwards[3], Mary James Cora[2] Edwards, William Archibald[1] Edwards) was born on 24 Dec 1928. She married Henry Wallace Meador on 15 Sep 1951.

Henry Wallace Meador and Jean Reid Skillern had the following children:

114. i. ANN SKILLERN[5] MEADOR was born on 14 Sep 1953 in Dallas County, Texas. She married MICHAEL RAY WILLIAMS.

115. ii. WILSON HENRY MEADOR was born on 11 Jan 1955 in Dallas County, Texas. He married KENDA MAYME NORTH.

 iii. JEAN HILL MEADOR was born on 18 Mar 1958 in Dallas County, Texas.

116. iv. JOHN RAE MEADOR was born on 02 Jun 1959 in Dallas County, Texas. He married TANYA LYNETTE CARLSON. She was born on 01 Jan 1962.

 v. THOMAS EDWARD MEADOR was born on 29 Aug 1969 in Dallas County, Texas.

58. **ROBERT SKILLERN[4] FOLSOM** (Zula[3] Skillern, Mary James Cora[2] Edwards, William Archibald[1] Edwards) was born on 15 Feb 1927 in Dallas County, Texas. He married Margaret Monnette Dalton on 07 Mar 1949 in Dallas, Texas.

More About Robert Skillern Folsom:
Occupation: Bet. 1964-1966; President of Dallas, Texas Independant School District
Board
Occupation: Bet. 1976-1981; Mayor of Dallas, Texas

Robert Skillern Folsom and Margaret Monnette Dalton had the following children:

117. i. MARGARET DIANE[5] FOLSOM was born on 14 May 1950 in Dallas County, Texas. She married WAYNE RALPH MILLER. She married ROBERT FRANK.

118. ii. DEBRA FOLSOM was born on 09 Nov 1953 in Dallas County, Texas. She married DON MICHAEL JARMA.

iii. JOHN VEST FOLSOM was born on 01 May 1956 in Dalllas County, Texas. He died on 30 May 1983. He married KAREN TOWNSEN.

119. iv. ROBERT STEPHEN FOLSOM was born on 02 Jan 1959 in Dallas County, Texas. He married SHARON MARIE ST. GERMAINE.

59. **WILLIAM EUGENE[4] WEATHERFORD** (Zola[3] Skillern, Mary James Cora[2] Edwards, William Archibald[1] Edwards) was born on 02 Jul 1928. He died on 20 Sep 1998 in Dallas County, Texas. He married **JUDITH WALLACE POLLARD**. He married **KAY HUGHES**.

William Eugene Weatherford and Judith Wallace Pollard had the following children:

120. i. WILLIAM SKILLERN[5] WEATHERFORD was born on 29 Aug 1951 in Dallas County, Texas. He married CATHY ANN WARNER.

ii. JULIA ANN WEATHERFORD was born on 10 Jul 1953 in Dallas County, Texas. She married MIKE SANDERS.

121. iii. MARK WALLACE WEATHERFORD was born on 22 Jul 1956 in Dallas County, Texas. He married STEPHANIE ANNE CATTANACH.

122. iv. MARY MARGARET WEATHERFORD was born on 11 Aug 1962 in Dallas County, Texas. She married JAMES MICHAEL NOLAN.

60. **LEROY MONROE[4] NAPIER** (Mary Evelyn[3] Skillern, Mary James Cora[2] Edwards, William Archibald[1] Edwards) was born on 18 Jun 1935 in Dallas County, Texas. He married **WILMA LEE FRANKLIN**. He married **BETTY PEARL BRADLEY**.

Leroy Monroe Napier and Wilma Lee Franklin had the following children:

i. STEPHEN WAYNE[5] NAPIER was born in 1962.

ii. BRYAN LEE NAPIER was born on 24 Jul 1964 in Dallas County, Texas.

Leroy Monroe Napier and Betty Pearl Bradley had the following children:

123. iii. GREGG LEE NAPIER was born in 1968. He married TAMARA JEAN AXTON.

124. iv. PAUL BRADLEY NAPIER was born in 1972. He married Jayme Lynn Hall in 1999.

125. v. STEVEN DALE NAPIER was born in 1979. He married Crystal McCormick in 2002.

61. **ROBERT DONALD[4] HANCOCK** (Jean[3] Skillern, Mary James Cora[2] Edwards, William Archibald[1] Edwards) was born on 31 Jan 1940 in Dallas County, Texas. He married **KAREN SUE DUGGAN**.

Robert Donald Hancock and Karen Sue Duggan had the following children:

126.   i.   GREGORY SCOTT[5] HANCOCK was born on 19 Oct 1966 in Dallas County, Texas. He married GISEL HERNANDEZ.

127.   ii.   MICHELE ELISE HANCOCK was born on 01 Aug 1971 in Dallas County, Texas. She married MICHAEL DAVID TOTH.

62.   ORPHIE[4] NEATHERY (Orphie Wilbur[3], Annie Lee[2] Edwards, William Archibald[1] Edwards) was born on 26 Apr 1912 in Haskell, Texas. He died on 15 Sep 1978. He married THELMA WINCHESTER. She was born on 01 May 1915. She died in Apr 1965.

Orphie Neathery and Thelma Winchester had the following child:

128.   i.   ORPHIE[5] NEATHERY was born on 09 Sep 1941 in Granite, Oklahoma. He married ANNETTE DARLENE OLIVE. She was born on 24 May 1940 in Mangum, Oklahoma.

63.   WILLIAM NEATHERY[4] LAMPE (Vera Ione[3] Neathery, Annie Lee[2] Edwards, William Archibald[1] Edwards) was born on 24 Jul 1926 in Amarillo, Texas. He married JIMMA JOANN DRAKE. She was born on 25 May 1929 in Hamlin, Texas.

William Neathery Lampe and Jimma Joann Drake had the following children:

129.   i.   LINDA LOUISE[5] LAMPE was born on 05 Mar 1953 in Amarillo, Texas. She married Carl Lynn Ingram on 08 Nov 1980 in Amarillo, Texas. He was born on 25 Mar 1952 in Hamlin, Texas.

130.   ii.   SALLY ANN LAMPE was born on 25 Feb 1955 in Amarillo, Texas. She married Charles Edward Boyd on 09 May 1979 in Amarillo, Texas. He was born on 18 Nov 1952 in St. Louis, Missouri.

     iii.   STEVEN DRAKE LAMPE was born on 25 Apr 1958 in Amarillo, Texas.

64.   ALMA RUTH[4] LAMPE (Vera Ione[3] Neathery, Annie Lee[2] Edwards, William Archibald[1] Edwards) was born on 07 Apr 1929 in Amarillo, Texas. She married JAMES RAY MCKENZIE. He was born on 14 Feb 1925 in Van, Texas.

James Ray McKenzie and Alma Ruth Lampe had the following children:

131.   i.   LAURA RUTH[5] MCKENZIE was born on 11 Apr 1959. She married Robin Duncan on 12 Aug 1979. He was born on 11 Apr 1957 in Amarillo, Texas.

132.   ii.   PATTI MCKENZIE was born on 09 Apr 1960. She married MARK EISENBURG.

65.   MARY ANN[4] ALEXANDER (Fay Edwina[3] Neathery, Annie Lee[2] Edwards, William Archibald[1] Edwards) was born on 22 Sep 1912 in Haskell, Texas. She married Eldon Luther Hill in Dec 1942 in Seymour, Texas.

Eldon Luther Hill and Mary Ann Alexander had the following child:

133.   i.   JANE ANN[5] HILL was born on 21 Feb 1947 in Dallas, Texas. She married PARKS WEYLAND BELL.

66.   EVELYN FAYE[4] ALEXANDER (Fay Edwina[3] Neathery, Annie Lee[2] Edwards, William Archibald[1] Edwards) was born on 15 Oct 1915 in Haskell, Texas. She died on 18 Mar 1984 in Quitman, Texas. She married Roy Stanley Lankford, son of Montiville Lankford and Roxanna Gorman on 03 Feb 1935 in Frederick, Oklahoma. He was born on 29 Jan 1909 in Seymour, Texas. He died on 21 May 1992 in Longview, Texas.

More About Roy Stanley Lankford:

Burial: Dallas, Texas

Roy Stanley Lankford and Evelyn Faye Alexander had the following children:

134. i. CAROL SUE[5] LANKFORD was born on 07 Dec 1937 in Wichita Falls, Texas. She died on 03 Sep 1996 in Longview, Texas. She married (1) JACK TINER, son of Ivory Tiner and Mabel Seale on 08 Aug 1958 in Dallas, Texas. He was born on 27 Jan 1936 in Dallas, Texas. She married (2) JACK RAMEY in Oct 1983.

135. ii. WALLACE WAYNE LANKFORD was born on 17 Nov 1948 in Dallas, Texas. He married (1) SUSAN JOHNSON on 26 Jun 1971 in Dallas County, Texas. She was born about 1949. He married (2) PEGGY WOODWARD MONTGOMERY on 26 May 1978 in Austin, Texas.

67. RUTH[4] ALEXANDER (Fay Edwina[3] Neathery, Annie Lee[2] Edwards, William Archibald[1] Edwards) was born on 14 Sep 1918 in Palestine, Texas. She married Thomas Woodard Smith on 17 Jan 1942 in Seymour, Texas. He was born on 13 Jul 1917 in Center, Texas. He died on 02 Oct 1980 in Austin, Texas.

Thomas Woodard Smith and Ruth Alexander had the following children:

136. i. THOMAS WOODARD[5] SMITH was born on 03 Aug 1943 in Shreveport, Louisiana. He married Jacqueline (unknown) on 21 Jun 1968 in Berkley, California.

137. ii. WILLIAM ALEXANDER SMITH was born on 25 Nov 1947. He married MIMI VAN BOSSUM.

138. iii. BEVERLY SUE SMITH was born on 30 Jan 1950 in Shreveport, Louisiana. She married Thomas Brian Dunn on 29 May 1971.

68. CONSTANCE[4] ALEXANDER (Fay Edwina[3] Neathery, Annie Lee[2] Edwards, William Archibald[1] Edwards) was born on 07 Jul 1923 in Seymour, Texas. She married (1) HARRY TAULMAN BOWERS on 09 Dec 1941 in Fort Worth, Texas. She married (2) FREDERICK P. STOCKMAN on 24 May 1977 in Los Angeles, California.

Harry Taulman Bowers and Constance Alexander had the following children:

139. i. HARRY TAULMAN[5] BOWERS was born on 30 Nov 1942 in Lufkin, Texas. He married JUDITH ANN VITELLO.

 ii. ROBBIE FAY BOWERS was born on 31 May 1944 in Dallas, Texas.

 iii. CLARINE BOWERS was born on 31 May 1944 in Dallas, Texas.

69. JOHN RICHARD[4] OATES (Deron Adelle[3] Neathery, Annie Lee[2] Edwards, William Archibald[1] Edwards) was born on 17 May 1914 in Haskell, Texas. He died on 27 Dec 1980 in Bell County, Texas. He married (1) LONELLE WHITAKER on 24 Nov 1938. He married JEFFIE MAE TURPEN. She was born on 10 Mar 1914 in Redford, Indiana.

John Richard Oates and Lonelle Whitaker had the following child:

140. i. JOHN RICHARD[5] OATES was born on 22 Sep 1946 in Abilene, Texas. He married Janice Marie Caldwell on 09 Jul 1966 in Bell County, Texas. She was born on 08 Oct 1947 in Taylor County, Texas.

John Richard Oates and Jeffie Mae Turpen had the following children:

 ii. OSCAR KENNETH OATES was born on 29 Sep 1950 in Abilene, Texas.

iii.   MARGARET DERON OATES was born on 26 Sep 1955 in Stamford, Texas.

70.   JENNY LEE[4] WITHERS (Shirley Lorene[3] Neathery, Annie Lee[2] Edwards, William Archibald[1] Edwards) was born on 05 Dec 1915 in Dallas, Texas. She married AMBRIS VETETO.

Ambris Veteto and Jenny Lee Withers had the following children:

141.   i.   ARTY BRUCE[5] VETETO was born on 12 Jul 1942 in San Diego, California. He married Jeanie Batchelor on 24 Apr 1971. She was born on 24 Mar 1947.

142.   ii.   SHIRLEY LULU VETETO was born on 14 Nov 1943 in National City, California. She married Ross Sutherland on 04 Mar 1967. He was born on 17 Oct 1942.

143.   iii.   GINGER VETETO was born on 26 Sep 1949 in Oceanside, California. She married Hans Munck on 26 Dec 1971. He was born on 21 Jan 1950.

    iv.   PEGGY VETETO was born on 26 Oct 1951 in Oceanside, California. She married Kevin Waide on 26 Jan 1979. He was born on 22 Feb 1952.

71.   NELDA LYNN[4] NEATHERY (Barney Lee[3], Annie Lee[2] Edwards, William Archibald[1] Edwards) was born on 13 Feb 1932. She married Russell Larry Robinson on 29 Aug 1953. He died in 1968.

Russell Larry Robinson and Nelda Lynn Neathery had the following child:

    i.   EDWARD ENGLAND[5] ROBINSON was born on 29 Nov 1963 in Wichita County, Texas.

72.   GLADYS ANN[4] NEATHERY (Barney Lee[3], Annie Lee[2] Edwards, William Archibald[1] Edwards) was born on 14 Feb 1934. She married MAX KING.

Max King and Gladys Ann Neathery had the following children:

    i.   LEE[5] KING was born on 26 Oct 1963.

    ii.   GLEN KING was born on 19 Dec 1965.

73.   JEANETTE LUCILLE[4] WEINERT (Elsa Lucille[3] Neathery, Annie Lee[2] Edwards, William Archibald[1] Edwards) was born on 24 Sep 1922 in Haskell, Texas. She married GEORGE J. ROEBER. He was born on 22 Jan 1921.

George J. Roeber and Jeanette Lucille Weinert had the following children:

144.   i.   DAVID GEORGE[5] ROEBER was born on 29 Aug 1946 in San Antonio, Texas. He married CHERYL ANDERSON.

145.   ii.   DANIEL WAYNE ROEBER was born on 14 Jul 1949. He married JEANIE MOORE.

146.   iii.   LUANNE ROEBER was born on 05 Dec 1952. She married STEVEN SCHUETZE.

74.   ANNIE LEE[4] WEINERT (Elsa Lucille[3] Neathery, Annie Lee[2] Edwards, William Archibald[1] Edwards) was born on 26 Apr 1926 in Weinert, Texas. She married DONALD E. WEISE. He was born on 29 Mar 1922.

Donald E. Weise and Annie Lee Weinert had the following child:

147.   i.   PATRICIA ANN[5] WEISE was born on 24 May 1947. She married EDWARD HAGEN.

75.   WILLIAM RICHARD[4] WEINERT (Elsa Lucille[3] Neathery, Annie Lee[2] Edwards, William Archibald[1] Edwards) was born on 18 Oct 1929 in Weinert, Texas. He married HAZEL CLAIRE TURNER.

William Richard Weinert and Hazel Claire Turner had the following child:

      i.   ROCHELLE RENEE[5] WEINERT was born on 07 Aug 1957. She married LESLIE NICKELIASON.

76.   CHARLES CLARENCE[4] CARTER (Dorothy[3] Lester, Willie Maud[2] Edwards, William Archibald[1] Edwards) was born on 14 Jul 1919 in Dallas, Dallas County, Texas. He died on 17 Mar 2002 in Plano, Texas. He married NELLIS RHEA DIXON. She was born on 20 Oct 1921 in Dallas, Dallas County, Texas. She died on 30 Aug 2005 in Plano, Texas.

More About Charles Clarence Carter:
Burial: 20 Mar 2002 in Restland Memorial Park, Dallas,
Texas Cause Of Death: Cereborovascular Hemorrhage
Occupation: Insurance Claims Adjuster

More About Nellis Rhea Dixon:
Burial: 02 Sep 2005 in Restland Memorial Park, Dallas,
Texas Cause Of Death: Congestive Heart Failure

Charles Clarence Carter and Nellis Rhea Dixon had the following child:

148.   i. CHARLES EUGENE[5] CARTER was born on 05 Oct 1952 in Dallas,Texas. He married Debra Elaine Meritt on 09 Jan 1981 in Tarrant County, Texas. She was born in 1960 in Texas.

77.   DOROTHY JUANITA[4] CARTER (Dorothy[3] Lester, Willie Maud[2] Edwards, William Archibald[1] Edwards) was born on 15 Nov 1920 in Dallas, Dallas County, Texas. She married PERRY IKE BLEVINS. He was born on 09 Jun 1914 in Holdenville, Huges County, Oklahoma. He died on 15 Apr 1996 in Fresno County, California.

Perry Ike Blevins and Dorothy Juanita Carter had the following child:

      i.   CHARLSIE VERLE[5] BLEVINS was born on 27 Nov 1940 in Tulare County, California.

78.   JOHN FRANKLIN[4] WILSON (William Henry[3], Carrie Louise[2] Edwards, William Archibald[1] Edwards) was born in Sherman, Texas. He married MARCELLENE ROBERTS SNORF. She was born in Chicago, Illinois.

John Franklin Wilson and Marcellene Roberts Snorf had the following children:

149.   i. MARCELLENE SNORF[5] WILSON was born on 02 Dec 1946 in Dallas County, Texas. She married STEPHEN HUNT SANDS.

      ii.   JOHN FRANKLIN WILSON was born on 16 Feb 1951 in Dallas, Texas.

150.   iii. DAVID SNORF WILSON was born on 19 Apr 1954 in Dallas County, Texas. He married DEBORAH LINDA FRY.

79.   EVELYN STORM[4] WILSON (William Henry[3], Carrie Louise[2] Edwards, William Archibald[1] Edwards) was born on 25 Nov 1915 in Sherman, Texas. She married WARREN EASTWOOD TRACY.

Warren Eastwood Tracy and Evelyn Storm Wilson had the following child:

      i.   WARREN FRANK[5] TRACY was born on 02 Sep 1942 in Harris county, Texas.

80.   JEAN RUTH[4] MCDANIEL (Carrie Winifred[3] Jones, Mattie Elizabeth[2] Edwards, William Archibald[1] Edwards) was born on 10 Feb 1924 in Handley, Texas. She married Harry Edward Ailey on 06 Jul 1942 in Dallas, Texas. He died on 11 Nov 1974.

More About Harry Edward Ailey:
Burial: Brownwood, Texas

Harry Edward Ailey and Jean Ruth McDaniel had the following child:

      i.   JANET ELIZABETH[5] AILEY was born on 21 Oct 1946 in Dallas, Texas. She married Tod D. Shampanore in Garland, Texas.

81.   **CHARLES CRAIG[4] WOODSON** (Marjory Ruth[3] Jones, Mattie Elizabeth[2] Edwards, William Archibald[1] Edwards) was born on 22 Oct 1933 in Palestine, Texas. He married Peggy Loraine Mayfield on 20 Jun 1953 in Waco, Texas.

Charles Craig Woodson and Peggy Loraine Mayfield had the following children:

      i.   LISA ELAINE[5] WOODSON was born on 16 Jun 1955 in Brownwood, Texas.

      ii.   LESLIE RUTH WOODSON was born on 24 Jun 1957 in Brownwood, Texas.

82.   **BEN JONES[4] WOODSON** (Marjory Ruth[3] Jones, Mattie Elizabeth[2] Edwards, William Archibald[1] Edwards) was born on 24 Nov 1934 in Palestine, Texas. He married (1) **DONI LOUISE RICHARDSON** on 27 Dec 1955 in Lamesa, Texas. He married (2) **SHIRLEY GREGORY BOYD** on 02 Jan 1975.

Ben Jones Woodson and Doni Louise Richardson had the following children:

151.   i.   BEN JONES[5] WOODSON was born on 10 Sep 1956 in Brownwood, Texas. He married SHARYN KAY FINEGAN.

152.   ii.   LAURILYN LOUISE WOODSON was born on 18 Jan 1959 in Del Norte, Colorado. She married STEVEN WAYNE BUILTA.

      iii. CHARLES LANCE WOODSON was born on 27 May 1970 in Del Rio, Texas.

Ben Jones Woodson and Shirley Gregory Boyd had the following child:

      iv. SHARLEE BROOKS WOODSON was born on 17 Mar 1977 in Houston, Texas.

83.   **JOHN ROSS[4] WOODSON** (Marjory Ruth[3] Jones, Mattie Elizabeth[2] Edwards, William Archibald[1] Edwards) was born on 19 Mar 1938 in Dallas, Texas. He married Jo Alice Moglia in Dec 1969 in Austin, Texas.

John Ross Woodson and Jo Alice Moglia had the following children:

      i.   TRACEY ANN[5] WOODSON was born on 23 Aug 1965 in Austin, Texas.

      ii.   JOHN BRADY WOODSON was born on 31 May 1968 in Austin, Texas.

      iii. ASHLEY CHRISTINE WOODSON was born on 02 Dec 1969 in Austin, Texas.

84.   **CAROL ANN[4] JONES** (Robert Winton[3], Mattie Elizabeth[2] Edwards, William Archibald[1] Edwards) was born on 14 Sep 1930 in Dallas, Texas. She married Ira DuBois Johnson on 14 Aug 1954. He died about 1976.

Ira DuBois Johnson and Carol Ann Jones had the following child:

      i.   CLAY DUBOIS[5] JOHNSON was born on 03 Jul 1956 in Lexington, Virginia.

Generation 5

85.   **LELA PATRICIA[5] CONNALLY** (Robert Edwards[4], Clara Lillian[3] Edwards, Theophilus Ambrose[2] Edwards, William Archibald[1] Edwards) was born on 07 Mar 1930 in Houston, Texas. She married

(1) **Earl Leon Wingo** on 23 Jul 1947 in Andalusia, Alabama. He was born on 03 Jul 1931 in Hattiesburg, Mississippi. She married (2) **Clark H. Gilliland** on 21 Jul 1971. She married **Dennis T. Barrow**.

Earl Leon Wingo and Lela Patricia Connally had the following children:

153.   i.   **Earl Leon**[6] **Wingo** was born on 22 Oct 1948 in Andalusia, Alabama. He married Candice Johnson on 14 Dec 1974.

    ii.   **Michael Wingo** was born on 21 Mar 1951 in Andalusia, Alabama.

    iii.   **Robert Powell Wingo** was born on 23 Jul 1954 in Andalusia, Alabama. He died in Aug 1975.

86.   **Robert Edwards**[5] **Connally** (Robert Edwards[4], Clara Lillian[3] Edwards, Theophilus Ambrose[2] Edwards, William Archibald[1] Edwards) was born on 16 Nov 1931 in Dallas, Texas. He died on 06 Feb 1979. He married Frances Bullock on 09 Aug 1955.

Robert Edwards Connally and Frances Bullock had the following children:

    i.   **Sharan Amanda**[6] **Connally** was born on 29 Jul 1956.

    ii.   **Karen Sue Connally** was born on 11 Nov 1960.

    iii.   **Keith Edward Connally** was born on 06 Sep 1964.

87.   **Lillian**[5] **Connally** (Robert Edwards[4], Clara Lillian[3] Edwards, Theophilus Ambrose[2] Edwards, William Archibald[1] Edwards) was born on 19 Jul 1933 in Dallas, Texas. She married John William Renfro on 16 Apr 1952.

John William Renfro and Lillian Connally had the following children:

    i.   **Mary Debra**[6] **Renfro** was born on 01 Aug 1953.

    ii.   **John William Renfro**.

    iii.   **James Benjamin Renfro** was born on 04 Apr 1959.

88.   **Mary**[5] **Connally** (Robert Edwards[4], Clara Lillian[3] Edwards, Theophilus Ambrose[2] Edwards, William Archibald[1] Edwards) was born on 05 Nov 1936 in Montgomery, Alabama. She married Frank Garrett Daniel on 28 Dec 1955.

Frank Garrett Daniel and Mary Connally had the following children:

    i.   **Connie**[6] **Daniel** was born on 09 Sep 1956.

        Notes for Connie Daniel:
        Connie and Donna are twins.

    ii.   **Donna Daniel** was born on 09 Sep 1956.

        Notes for Donna Daniel:
        Donna and Connie are twins.

    iii.   **Mary Ann Daniel** was born on 18 Sep 1958.

    iv.   FRANK GARRET DANIEL was born on 20 Mar 1961.

89.   NANCY ANN[5] CONNALLY (Frank Leonard[4], Clara Lillian[3] Edwards, Theophilus Ambrose[2] Edwards, William Archibald[1] Edwards) was born on 13 Dec 1931. She married Bill Joe Houck on 02 Feb 1951.

Bill Joe Houck and Nancy Ann Connally had the following children:

    i.   CYNTHIA[6] HOUCK was born on 27 Dec 1952.

    ii.   JULIE ANN HOUCK was born on 04 Nov 1957 in Harris county, Texas.

    iii.   STEPHEN JOSEPH HOUCK was born on 18 Feb 1967 in Harris county, Texas.

90.   CLARA ANN[5] CONNALLY (James Marvin[4], Clara Lillian[3] Edwards, Theophilus Ambrose[2] Edwards, William Archibald[1] Edwards) was born on 10 Oct 1954. She married CHARLES WAYNE TOWNSON. Charles Wayne Townson and Clara Ann Connally had the following children:

    i.   DAVID WAYNE[6] TOWNSON was born on 16 Dec 1972 in Ellis County, Texas.

    ii.   CANDY ANN TOWNSON was born on 15 Sep 1976 in Dallas County, Texas.

91.   LEE OLIA[5] RODGERS (Nora Elizabeth[4] Troth, Laura Lee Olia[3] Edwards, Theophilus Ambrose[2] Edwards, William Archibald[1] Edwards) was born on 23 Oct 1945 in Dallas County, Texas. She married GLEN ARTHUR SALE.

Glen Arthur Sale and Lee Olia Rodgers had the following child:

    i.   JOY ELIZABETH[6] SALE was born on 31 Oct 1974 in Dallas County, Texas.

92.   ANN ELIZABETH[5] TROTH (Robert Weldford[4], Laura Lee Olia[3] Edwards, Theophilus Ambrose[2] Edwards, William Archibald[1] Edwards) was born on 03 Sep 1948 in Dallas County, Texas. She married Michael Mottern Coleman on 27 Jun 1969. He was born on 27 Dec 1946 in Pomona, California.

Michael Mottern Coleman and Ann Elizabeth Troth had the following child:

    i.   TERI JOY[6] COLEMAN was born on 13 Sep 1978 in Ozark, Alabama.

93.   JANE FRANCES[5] TROTH (Robert Weldford[4], Laura Lee Olia[3] Edwards, Theophilus Ambrose[2] Edwards, William Archibald[1] Edwards) was born on 16 Nov 1950 in Dallas County, Texas. She married Richard Cummings McCorkle on 17 Jul 1971. He was born on 22 Mar 1950 in Dallas, Texas.

Richard Cummings McCorkle and Jane Frances Troth had the following child:

    i.   KEELEY JANE[6] MCCORKLE was born on 21 Sep 1975 in Dallas, Texas.

94.   LINDA ANN[5] MULLANE (Rosemary[4] Troth, Laura Lee Olia[3] Edwards, Theophilus Ambrose[2] Edwards, William Archibald[1] Edwards) was born on 05 May 1948 in Dallas County, Texas. She married ROGER HUGHES KLINE. He was born on 16 May 1945 in Evanston, Illinois.

Roger Hughes Kline and Linda Ann Mullane had the following children:

    i.   CHAD NATHAN[6] KLINE was born on 06 Nov 1973 in Dallas, Texas.

    ii.   AMY ELIZABETH KLINE was born on 20 Feb 1975 in Dallas, Texas.

    iii.   DOUGLAS AARON KLINE was born on 04 Jan 1979 in Dallas, Texas.

    iv.   JOHN ROBERT MULLANE was born on 21 Jul 1955 in Dallas, Texas.

Notes for John Robert Mullane:

John Robert Mullane was adopted.

95.   **SUSAN LEE**[5] **DAVENPORT** (Barbara Ruth[4] Troth, Laura Lee Olia[3] Edwards, Theophilus Ambrose[2] Edwards, William Archibald[1] Edwards) was born on 15 Aug 1952 in Dallas County, Texas. She married Roy Michael Thomas on 14 Jun 1975. He was born on 15 Jul 1952 in Dallas, Texas.

Roy Michael Thomas and Susan Lee Davenport had the following child:

    i.   RICHARD MICHAEL[6] THOMAS was born on 15 Nov 1978 in Dallas, Texas.

96.   **GEORGE MARVIN**[5] **EDWARDS** (Theophilus Marvin[4], Theophilus Marvin[3], Theophilus Ambrose[2], William Archibald[1]) was born on 16 Jun 1953 in Dallas County, Texas. He married Patti Susan Rush on 10 Mar 1979 in Dallas, Texas.

George Marvin Edwards and Patti Susan Rush had the following children:

    i.   NORA AMBER[6] EDWARDS was born on 04 Jul 1981 in Dallas County, Texas.

    ii.   ROBIN KATHLEEN EDWARDS was born on 13 Sep 1984 in Dallas County, Texas.

    iii.   GEORGE MARVIN EDWARDS was born on 27 Sep 1988 in Dallas County, Texas.

97.   **CHARLES AUSTIN**[5] **EDWARDS** (Theophilus Marvin[4], Theophilus Marvin[3], Theophilus Ambrose[2], William Archibald[1]) was born on 13 Jan 1955 in Dallas, Texas. He married **ROMALDA ANN ALLSUP**.

Charles Austin Edwards and Romalda Ann Allsup had the following children:

    i.   SYLVIA LLOYD ALLSUP[6] EDWARDS was born on 09 Jan 1986 in Travis County, Texas.

    ii.   NEEKA SLOAN ALLSUP EDWARDS was born on 13 Jan 1988 in Travis County, Texas.

    iii.   NATALIE CORINNE ALLSUP EDWARDS was born on 31 Oct 1989 in Travis County, Texas.

98.   **EVANS MOORE**[5] **CLEMENTS** (Frances Jane[4] Edwards, Theophilus Marvin[3] Edwards, Theophilus Ambrose[2] Edwards, William Archibald[1] Edwards) was born on 21 May 1941 in Nashville, Tennessee. He married Harriet Vasti Greene on 19 Mar 1960 in Nashville, Tennessee. She was born on 21 Jan 1943.

Evans Moore Clements and Harriet Vasti Greene had the following children:

    i.   EVANS MOORE[6] CLEMENTS was born on 21 Dec 1960.

    ii.   CAROLINE ASHLEY CLEMENTS was born on 07 Apr 1967.

99.   **JANE EDWARDS**[5] **CLEMENTS** (Frances Jane[4] Edwards, Theophilus Marvin[3] Edwards, Theophilus Ambrose[2] Edwards, William Archibald[1] Edwards) was born on 08 Oct 1942 in Nashville, Tennessee. She married David Wilson McMackin on 19 Jan 1963 in Nashville, Tennessee. He was born on 06 Dec 1937.

David Wilson McMackin and Jane Edwards Clements had the following children:

    i.   DAVID WILSON[6] MCMACKIN was born on 16 Mar 1964.

    ii.   RICHARD CLEMENTS MCMACKIN was born on 29 Jun 1966.

100.   **MARVIN EDWARDS**[5] **CLEMENTS** (Frances Jane[4] Edwards, Theophilus Marvin[3] Edwards, Theophilus Ambrose[2] Edwards, William Archibald[1] Edwards) was born on 21 Feb 1945 in Nashville, Tennessee. He married Patricia Martin on 20 Aug 1966. She was born on 18 Apr 1946.

Marvin Edwards Clements and Patricia Martin had the following children:

    i.   MARVIN EDWARDS[6] CLEMENTS was born on 29 Oct 1967.

    ii.   SCOTT MARTIN CLEMENTS was born on 25 Sep 1971.

101.   **BARBARA EDWARDS**[5] **DURST** (Katherine Ann[4] Edwards, Theophilus Marvin[3] Edwards, Theophilus Ambrose[2] Edwards, William Archibald[1] Edwards) was born on 13 May 1942. She married Robert Hunter McLean on 22 Jun 1963. He was born on 26 Apr 1941.

Robert Hunter McLean and Barbara Edwards Durst had the following children:

    i.   KELLY DURST[6] MCLEAN was born on 25 Sep 1966.

    ii.   HUNTER THORNE MCLEAN was born on 03 Jul 1968.

    iii.   MARK BEALL MCLEAN was born on 13 Jul 1971.

102.   **CYNTHIA ELIZABETH**[5] **DAVIS** (Margy Lee[4] Robertson, Ruby Elizabeth[3] Edwards, Theophilus Ambrose[2] Edwards, William Archibald[1] Edwards) was born on 01 Mar 1946 in Dallas County, Texas. She married Ronald L. Giles on 12 May 1965. He was born on 07 Apr 1943.

Ronald L. Giles and Cynthia Elizabeth Davis had the following children:

    i.   CHRISTOPHER EDWARDS[6] GILES was born on 01 Mar 1966.

    ii.   JOSHUA MATTHEW GILES was born on 17 Sep 1970.

103.   **CHRISTOPHER LEE**[5] **SKILLERN** (Frank Lloyd[4], Frank Lloyd[3], Mary James Cora[2] Edwards, William Archibald[1] Edwards) was born on 30 Jun 1941 in Dallas County, Texas. He married **SANDRA KISH**. Christopher Lee Skillern and Sandra Kish had the following children:

    i.   CHRISTOPHER SHAWN[6] SKILLERN was born in 1968.

    ii.   KERRIN EILEEN SKILLERN was born in 1970.

104.   **ELIZABETH PEYTON**[5] **SKILLERN** (Frank Lloyd[4], Frank Lloyd[3], Mary James Cora[2] Edwards, William Archibald[1] Edwards) was born on 30 Jan 1944 in Cameron County, Texas. She married **ROBERT HAGERTY**.

Robert Hagerty and Elizabeth Peyton Skillern had the following children:

    i.   KATHERINE[6] HAGERTY was born in 1969.

    ii.   SCOTT FREDERICK HAGERTY was born in 1973.

105.   **EDWARD PRESTON**[5] **SNEED** (Mary Ann[4] Cofer, Edna Cora[3] Skillern, Mary James Cora[2] Edwards, William Archibald[1] Edwards) was born on 01 Mar 1947 in Dallas County, Texas. He married **BARBARA ALLEN HENRY**.

Edward Preston Sneed and Barbara Allen Henry had the following children:

      i.   MALIA ALLEN[6] SNEED was born on 21 Feb 1970 in Dallas County, Texas.

      ii.   GARTH EDWARD SNEED was born on 21 Aug 1972 in Dallas County, Texas.

      iii. EMILY CAROL SNEED was born on 12 Feb 1974 in Dallas County, Texas.

      iv. KIRK ALVIN SNEED was born on 12 Feb 1974 in Dallas County, Texas.

106.   **CAROL JOY[5] COFER** (William Frank[4], Edna Cora[3] Skillern, Mary James Cora[2] Edwards, William Archibald[1] Edwards) was born on 04 May 1950 in Dallas County, Texas. She married Loyd Frank Lewellen on 18 Mar 1967 in Dallas County, Texas.

Loyd Frank Lewellen and Carol Joy Cofer had the following children:

154.   i. LLOYD DANIEL[6] LEWELLEN was born on 11 Aug 1967 in Dallas County, Texas. He married JONI SUE HAMMER. She was born on 08 Dec 1967.

      ii.   JENNIFER LYNN LEWELLEN was born on 12 Feb 1971 in Dallas County, Texas.

107.   **JANET LEE[5] COFER** (William Frank[4], Edna Cora[3] Skillern, Mary James Cora[2] Edwards, William Archibald[1] Edwards) was born on 15 Dec 1951 in Dallas County, Texas. She married **DAN THOMAS BOATRIGHT**.

Dan Thomas Boatright and Janet Lee Cofer had the following children:

      i.   KELLIE MARIE[6] BOATRIGHT was born on 03 Feb 1979 in Dallas County, Texas.

      ii.   LESLIE KRISTEN BOATRIGHT was born on 20 Aug 1981 in Dallas County, Texas.

      iii. KENT THOMAS BOATRIGHT was born on 30 Oct 1986 in Dallas County, Texas.

108.   **CYNTHIA ANN[5] COFER** (William Frank[4], Edna Cora[3] Skillern, Mary James Cora[2] Edwards, William Archibald[1] Edwards) was born on 22 Jul 1955 in Dallas County, Texas. She married **MICHAEL LYNN WALL**.

Michael Lynn Wall and Cynthia Ann Cofer had the following children:

      i.   DUSTIN MICHAEL[6] WALL was born on 21 Jul 1981 in Dallas County, Texas.

      ii.   NATALIE MICHELE WALL was born on 07 Sep 1983 in Dallas County, Texas.

      iii. TRENTON RANIER WALL was born on 14 Feb 1986 in Dallas County, Texas.

109.   **WILLIAM FRANK[5] COFER** (William Frank[4], Edna Cora[3] Skillern, Mary James Cora[2] Edwards, William Archibald[1] Edwards) was born on 09 Nov 1961 in Dallas County, Texas. He married **CYNTHIA KAYE COLLINS**.

William Frank Cofer and Cynthia Kaye Collins had the following children:

      i.   MORGAN ALEXIA[6] COFER was born on 18 Sep 1988 in Dallas County, Texas.

      ii.   ERICA LEIGH COFER was born on 26 Sep 1990 in Dallas County, Texas.

      iii. COLLEEN REGAN COFER was born on 02 Jul 1992 in Dallas County, Texas.

110. **John Charles**[5] **Pope** (Mary Sue[4] Peterson, Lida[3] Skillern, Mary James Cora[2] Edwards, William Archibald[1] Edwards) was born on 22 Feb 1951 in Dallas County, Texas. He married **Sharon Evon Soladay**. She was born on 28 Oct 1948 in Taylor County, Texas.

John Charles Pope and Sharon Evon Soladay had the following children:

    i.   Jimmie Charles[6] Pope was born on 10 Dec 1972 in Tarrant County, Texas.

    ii.   Jared Skillern Pope was born on 14 Oct 1977 in Dallas County, Texas.

    iii.   Zachary Stephenson Pope was born on 14 Oct 1977 in Dallas County, Texas.

111. **Sam Skillern**[5] **Leake** (Betty Edwards[4] Skillern, Rae Edwards[3] Skillern, Mary James Cora[2] Edwards, William Archibald[1] Edwards) was born on 04 Oct 1941 in Dallas County, Texas. He married **Katharine Severance Sears**.

Sam Skillern Leake and Katharine Severance Sears had the following children:

    i.   Sam Skillern[6] Leake was born on 09 Aug 1968 in Dallas County, Texas.

    ii.   John Sears Leake was born on 09 Jul 1970 in Dallas County, Texas.

    iii.   Michael Wilson Leake was born on 08 Nov 1972 in Dallas County, Texas.

    iv.   David Russell Leake was born on 05 Jan 1978 in Dallas County, Texas.

112. **John Wilson**[5] **Leake** (Betty Edwards[4] Skillern, Rae Edwards[3] Skillern, Mary James Cora[2] Edwards, William Archibald[1] Edwards) was born on 25 Dec 1948 in Dallas County, Texas. He married **Maryann Wighaman**.

John Wilson Leake and Maryann Wighaman had the following child:

    i.   John Daniel[6] Leake was born on 05 Dec 1979 in Dallas County, Texas.

113. **Rae Skillern**[5] **Korn** (Anne Rae[4] Skillern, Rae Edwards[3] Skillern, Mary James Cora[2] Edwards, William Archibald[1] Edwards) was born on 01 Nov 1944 in Dallas County, Texas. He married **Donna Lynn Speigel**. He married **Brenda Ann Maddox**.

Rae Skillern Korn and Donna Lynn Speigel had the following children:

    i.   Donald Skillern[6] Korn was born on 01 Dec 1965 in Dallas County, Texas.

    ii.   Patrick Rae Korn was born on 16 Feb 1968 in Dallas County, Texas.

Rae Skillern Korn and Brenda Ann Maddox had the following child:

    iii.   Kent Rae Korn was born on 23 Dec 1984 in Dallas County, Texas.

114. **Ann Skillern**[5] **Meador** (Jean Reid[4] Skillern, Rae Edwards[3] Skillern, Mary James Cora[2] Edwards, William Archibald[1] Edwards) was born on 14 Sep 1953 in Dallas County, Texas. She married **Michael Ray Williams**.

Michael Ray Williams and Ann Skillern Meador had the following children:

    i.   Emma Louise Harris[6] Williams was born on 21 May 1989 in Dallas County, Texas.

    ii.   Hannah Marie Williams was born on 30 Mar 1994 in Dallas County, Texas.

115. **Wilson Henry**[5] **Meador** (Jean Reid[4] Skillern, Rae Edwards[3] Skillern, Mary James Cora[2] Edwards,

William Archibald[1] Edwards) was born on 11 Jan 1955 in Dallas County, Texas. He married **KENDA MAYME NORTH**.

Wilson Henry Meador and Kenda Mayme North had the following child:

    i.   DARYL CELESTE[6] MEADOR was born on 28 Feb 1990 in Dallas County, Texas.

116.   **JOHN RAE[5] MEADOR** (Jean Reid[4] Skillern, Rae Edwards[3] Skillern, Mary James Cora[2] Edwards, William Archibald[1] Edwards) was born on 02 Jun 1959 in Dallas County, Texas. He married **TANYA LYNETTE CARLSON**. She was born on 01 Jan 1962.

John Rae Meador and Tanya Lynette Carlson had the following children:

    i.   MATTHEW RAE[6] MEADOR was born on 06 Sep 1989 in Dallas County, Texas.

    ii.   WILLIAM HENRY MEADOR was born on 12 Mar 1992 in Dallas County, Texas.

117.   **MARGARET DIANE[5] FOLSOM** (Robert Skillern[4], Zula[3] Skillern, Mary James Cora[2] Edwards, William Archibald[1] Edwards) was born on 14 May 1950 in Dallas County, Texas. She married **WAYNE RALPH MILLER**. She married **ROBERT FRANK**.

Wayne Ralph Miller and Margaret Diane Folsom had the following children:

    i.   MARGARET DEBORAH[6] MILLER was born on 12 Aug 1980 in Dallas County, Texas.

    ii.   CLAYTON CARROLL MILLER was born in 1977.

118.   **DEBRA[5] FOLSOM** (Robert Skillern[4], Zula[3] Skillern, Mary James Cora[2] Edwards, William Archibald[1] Edwards) was born on 09 Nov 1953 in Dallas County, Texas. She married **DON MICHAEL JARMA**.

Don Michael Jarma and Debra Folsom had the following children:

    i.   HOLLY DIANE[6] JARMA was born on 20 Dec 1982 in Dallas County, Texas.

    ii.   CASEY MICHELLE JARMA was born on 05 Apr 1986 in Dallas County, Texas.

    iii.   JULIE JEANEAL JARMA was born on 01 Nov 1988 in Dallas County, Texas.

119.   **ROBERT STEPHEN[5] FOLSOM** (Robert Skillern[4], Zula[3] Skillern, Mary James Cora[2] Edwards, William Archibald[1] Edwards) was born on 02 Jan 1959 in Dallas County, Texas. He married **SHARON MARIE ST. GERMAINE**.

Robert Stephen Folsom and Sharon Marie St. Germaine had the following child:

    i.   HUNTER EUGENIA[6] FOLSOM was born on 18 May 1994 in Dallas County, Texas.

120.   **WILLIAM SKILLERN[5] WEATHERFORD** (William Eugene[4], Zola[3] Skillern, Mary James Cora[2] Edwards, William Archibald[1] Edwards) was born on 29 Aug 1951 in Dallas County, Texas. He married **CATHY ANN WARNER**.

William Skillern Weatherford and Cathy Ann Warner had the following children:

    i.   JACQUELINE MARIE[6] WEATHERFORD was born on 22 Mar 1978 in Dallas County, Texas.

    ii.   WILLIAM WARNER WEATHERFORD was born on 14 Nov 1979 in Dallas County, Texas.

    iii.   SAMUEL WALLACE WEATHERFORD was born on 29 Mar 1983 in Dallas County, Texas.

    iv.   ANDREW SKILLERN WEATHERFORD was born on 22 Jun 1985 in Dallas County, Texas.

    v.   GRACE ANN WEATHERFORD was born on 16 Aug 1986 in Dallas County, Texas.

121.   MARK WALLACE[5] WEATHERFORD (William Eugene[4], Zola[3] Skillern, Mary James Cora[2] Edwards, William Archibald[1] Edwards) was born on 22 Jul 1956 in Dallas County, Texas. He married STEPHANIE ANNE CATTANACH.

Mark Wallace Weatherford and Stephanie Anne Cattanach had the following children:

    i.   ROBERT WALLACE[6] WEATHERFORD was born on 10 Jul 1986 in Dallas County, Texas.

    ii.   CHARLOTTE ANN WEATHERFORD was born on 11 Jan 1990 in Dallas County, Texas.

122.   MARY MARGARET[5] WEATHERFORD (William Eugene[4], Zola[3] Skillern, Mary James Cora[2] Edwards, William Archibald[1] Edwards) was born on 11 Aug 1962 in Dallas County, Texas. She married JAMES MICHAEL NOLAN.

James Michael Nolan and Mary Margaret Weatherford had the following children:

    i.   GEORGIA WEATHERFORD[6] NOLAN was born on 25 Nov 1994 in Dallas County, Texas.

    ii.   JAMES MICHAEL NOLAN was born on 25 May 1989 in Dallas County, Texas.

    iii.   MARY MARGARET NOLAN was born on 25 Jan 1997 in Dallas County, Texas.

123.   GREGG LEE[5] NAPIER (Leroy Monroe[4], Mary Evelyn[3] Skillern, Mary James Cora[2] Edwards, William Archibald[1] Edwards) was born in 1968. He married TAMARA JEAN AXTON.
Gregg Lee Napier and Tamara Jean Axton had the following children:

    i.   RYAN RAY[6] NAPIER was born in 1989.

    ii.   ASHLEE NICHOLE NAPIER was born in 1993.

124.   PAUL BRADLEY[5] NAPIER (Leroy Monroe[4], Mary Evelyn[3] Skillern, Mary James Cora[2] Edwards, William Archibald[1] Edwards) was born in 1972. He married Jayme Lynn Hall in 1999.
Paul Bradley Napier and Jayme Lynn Hall had the following children:

    i.   BRADLEY CADE[6] NAPIER was born in 2002.

    ii.   BRENNA LYNN NAPIER was born in 2006.

125.   STEVEN DALE[5] NAPIER (Leroy Monroe[4], Mary Evelyn[3] Skillern, Mary James Cora[2] Edwards, William Archibald[1] Edwards) was born in 1979. He married Crystal McCormick in 2002.
Steven Dale Napier and Crystal McCormick had the following child:

    i.   HANNAH LEIGH ANN[6] NAPIER was born in 2006.

126.   GREGORY SCOTT[5] HANCOCK (Robert Donald[4], Jean[3] Skillern, Mary James Cora[2] Edwards, William Archibald[1] Edwards) was born on 19 Oct 1966 in Dallas County, Texas. He married GISEL HERNANDEZ.

Gregory Scott Hancock and Gisel Hernandez had the following child:

      i.   NICOLE ELISE[6] HANCOCK was born on 12 Oct 1991 in Harris county, Texas.

127.   **MICHELE ELISE**[5] **HANCOCK** (Robert Donald[4], Jean[3] Skillern, Mary James Cora[2] Edwards, William Archibald[1] Edwards) was born on 01 Aug 1971 in Dallas County, Texas. She married **MICHAEL DAVID TOTH**.

Michael David Toth and Michele Elise Hancock had the following child:

      i.   ASHLEY MORGAN[6] TOTH was born on 10 Jan 1997 in Harris county, Texas.

128.   **ORPHIE**[5] **NEATHERY** (Orphie[4], Orphie Wilbur[3], Annie Lee[2] Edwards, William Archibald[1] Edwards) was born on 09 Sep 1941 in Granite, Oklahoma. He married **ANNETTE DARLENE OLIVE**. She was born on 24 May 1940 in Mangum, Oklahoma.

Orphie Neathery and Annette Darlene Olive had the following children:

      i.   JEFFREY STEPHEN[6] NEATHERY was born on 07 Jan 1962 in Bryan, Texas.

      ii.   CONSTANCE ANNETTE NEATHERY was born on 10 Jul 1965 in Ganada, Texas.

129.   **LINDA LOUISE**[5] **LAMPE** (William Neathery[4], Vera Ione[3] Neathery, Annie Lee[2] Edwards, William Archibald[1] Edwards) was born on 05 Mar 1953 in Amarillo, Texas. She married Carl Lynn Ingram on 08 Nov 1980 in Amarillo, Texas. He was born on 25 Mar 1952 in Hamlin, Texas.

Carl Lynn Ingram and Linda Louise Lampe had the following children:

      i.   AUSTIN WILLIAM[6] INGRAM was born on 07 Jun 1982 in Bexar County, Texas.

      ii.   STEPHANIE ANNE INGRAM was born on 26 Mar 1986 in Bexar County, Texas.

      iii. LESLIE LEIGH INGRAM was born on 01 May 1990 in Bexar County, Texas.

130.   **SALLY ANN**[5] **LAMPE** (William Neathery[4], Vera Ione[3] Neathery, Annie Lee[2] Edwards, William Archibald[1] Edwards) was born on 25 Feb 1955 in Amarillo, Texas. She married Charles Edward Boyd on 09 May 1979 in Amarillo, Texas. He was born on 18 Nov 1952 in St. Louis, Missouri.

Charles Edward Boyd and Sally Ann Lampe had the following children:

      i.   STEPHEN BLAKE[6] BOYD was born on 21 May 1985 in Travis County, Texas.

      ii.   KELLY BLAIR BOYD was born on 19 Apr 1989 in Travis County, Texas.

131.   **LAURA RUTH**[5] **MCKENZIE** (Alma Ruth[4] Lampe, Vera Ione[3] Neathery, Annie Lee[2] Edwards, William Archibald[1] Edwards) was born on 11 Apr 1959. She married Robin Duncan on 12 Aug 1979. He was born on 11 Apr 1957 in Amarillo, Texas.

Robin Duncan and Laura Ruth McKenzie had the following child:

      i.   JAMIE DENISE[6] DUNCAN was born on 12 Aug 1980 in Potter County, Texas.

132.   **PATTI**[5] **MCKENZIE** (Alma Ruth[4] Lampe, Vera Ione[3] Neathery, Annie Lee[2] Edwards, William Archibald[1] Edwards) was born on 09 Apr 1960. She married **MARK EISENBURG**.

Mark Eisenburg and Patti McKenzie had the following child:

      i.   JENNIFER[6] EISENBURG was born on 19 Jul 1980.

133.   **JANE ANN**[5] **HILL** (Mary Ann[4] Alexander, Fay Edwina[3] Neathery, Annie Lee[2] Edwards, William Archibald[1] Edwards) was born on 21 Feb 1947 in Dallas, Texas. She married **PARKS WEYLAND**

BELL.

Parks Weyland Bell and Jane Ann Hill had the following child:
> i. JOSHUA HILL[6] BELL was born on 05 Jan 1980 in Dallas, Texas.

134. **CAROL SUE**[5] **LANKFORD** (Evelyn Faye[4] Alexander, Fay Edwina[3] Neathery, Annie Lee[2] Edwards, William Archibald[1] Edwards) was born on 07 Dec 1937 in Wichita Falls, Texas. She died on 03 Sep 1996 in Longview, Texas. She married (1) **JACK TINER**, son of Ivory Tiner and Mabel Seale on 08 Aug 1958 in Dallas, Texas. He was born on 27 Jan 1936 in Dallas, Texas. She married (2) **JACK RAMEY** in Oct 1983.

More About Carol Sue Lankford:
Burial: Judson, Texas

Jack Tiner and Carol Sue Lankford had the following child:
> 155. i. KELLIE RENE[6] TINER was born on 19 Nov 1962 in Dallas, Texas. She married (1) GREGG EMMANUEL TURNER, son of Baxter Turner and Bobbie Roberts on 02 Apr 1984 in Longview, Texas. He was born on 25 Dec 1962 in Mesquite, Texas. She married KENNETH RAY SEGERS. He was born on 28 Apr 1962.

135. **WALLACE WAYNE**[5] **LANKFORD** (Evelyn Faye[4] Alexander, Fay Edwina[3] Neathery, Annie Lee[2] Edwards, William Archibald[1] Edwards) was born on 17 Nov 1948 in Dallas, Texas. He married (1) **SUSAN JOHNSON** on 26 Jun 1971 in Dallas County, Texas. She was born about 1949. He married (2) **PEGGY WOODWARD MONTGOMERY** on 26 May 1978 in Austin, Texas.

Wallace Wayne Lankford and Peggy Woodward Montgomery had the following child:
> i. NATHAN WALLACE[6] LANKFORD was born on 16 Jan 1980.

136. **THOMAS WOODARD**[5] **SMITH** (Ruth[4] Alexander, Fay Edwina[3] Neathery, Annie Lee[2] Edwards, William Archibald[1] Edwards) was born on 03 Aug 1943 in Shreveport, Louisiana. He married Jacqueline (unknown) on 21 Jun 1968 in Berkley, California.

Thomas Woodard Smith and Jacqueline (unknown) had the following children:
> i. GABRIEL THOMAS[6] SMITH was born on 15 Nov 1969.
>
> ii. NEATHERY ELLEN SMITH was born on 05 May 1973.

137. **WILLIAM ALEXANDER**[5] **SMITH** (Ruth[4] Alexander, Fay Edwina[3] Neathery, Annie Lee[2] Edwards, William Archibald[1] Edwards) was born on 25 Nov 1947. He married **MIMI VAN BOSSUM**.
William Alexander Smith and Mimi Van Bossum had the following child:
> i. JAKE[6] SMITH.

138. **BEVERLY SUE**[5] **SMITH** (Ruth[4] Alexander, Fay Edwina[3] Neathery, Annie Lee[2] Edwards, William Archibald[1] Edwards) was born on 30 Jan 1950 in Shreveport, Louisiana. She married Thomas Brian Dunn on 29 May 1971.

Thomas Brian Dunn and Beverly Sue Smith had the following children:
> i. CASEY CLAYTON[6] DUNN was born on 21 Jun 1981 in Travis County, Texas.
>
> ii. AVERY LOUISE DUNN was born on 01 Aug 1985 in Travis County, Texas.

139. **HARRY TAULMAN**[5] **BOWERS** (Constance[4] Alexander, Fay Edwina[3] Neathery, Annie Lee[2] Edwards,

William Archibald[1] Edwards) was born on 30 Nov 1942 in Lufkin, Texas. He married JUDITH ANN VITELLO.

Harry Taulman Bowers and Judith Ann Vitello had the following child:

    i.   HARRY TAULMAN[6] BOWERS was born on 01 Feb 1974.

140.   **JOHN RICHARD[5] OATES** (John Richard[4], Deron Adelle[3] Neathery, Annie Lee[2] Edwards, William Archibald[1] Edwards) was born on 22 Sep 1946 in Abilene, Texas. He married Janice Marie Caldwell on 09 Jul 1966 in Bell County, Texas. She was born on 08 Oct 1947 in Taylor County, Texas.

John Richard Oates and Janice Marie Caldwell had the following children:

156.   i. LESLIE CAROL[6] OATES was born on 02 Mar 1967 in Lubbock, Texas. She married ROBERT ERNEST ANDERSON. He was born on 12 Sep 1965 in McLennan County, Texas.

    ii.   DAVID NELSON OATES was born on 29 Mar 1972 in Dallas, Texas.

141.   **ARTY BRUCE[5] VETETO** (Jenny Lee[4] Withers, Shirley Lorene[3] Neathery, Annie Lee[2] Edwards, William Archibald[1] Edwards) was born on 12 Jul 1942 in San Diego, California. He married Jeanie Batchelor on 24 Apr 1971. She was born on 24 Mar 1947.

Arty Bruce Veteto and Jeanie Batchelor had the following children:

    i.   TONY[6] VETETO was born on 04 Mar 1973.

    ii.   JOSHUA VETETO was born on 23 Dec 1976.

142.   **SHIRLEY LULU[5] VETETO** (Jenny Lee[4] Withers, Shirley Lorene[3] Neathery, Annie Lee[2] Edwards, William Archibald[1] Edwards) was born on 14 Nov 1943 in National City, California. She married Ross Sutherland on 04 Mar 1967. He was born on 17 Oct 1942.

Ross Sutherland and Shirley Lulu Veteto had the following child:

    i.   SCOTT[6] SUTHERLAND was born on 09 Apr 1975.

143.   **GINGER[5] VETETO** (Jenny Lee[4] Withers, Shirley Lorene[3] Neathery, Annie Lee[2] Edwards, William Archibald[1] Edwards) was born on 26 Sep 1949 in Oceanside, California. She married Hans Munck on 26 Dec 1971. He was born on 21 Jan 1950.

Hans Munck and Ginger Veteto had the following child:

    i.   STACEY[6] MUNCK was born on 24 Jun 1976.

144.   **DAVID GEORGE[5] ROEBER** (Jeanette Lucille[4] Weinert, Elsa Lucille[3] Neathery, Annie Lee[2] Edwards, William Archibald[1] Edwards) was born on 29 Aug 1946 in San Antonio, Texas. He married CHERYL ANDERSON.

David George Roeber and Cheryl Anderson had the following child:

    i.   SHANNON[6] ROEBER was born in Dec 1971.

145.   **DANIEL WAYNE[5] ROEBER** (Jeanette Lucille[4] Weinert, Elsa Lucille[3] Neathery, Annie Lee[2] Edwards, William Archibald[1] Edwards) was born on 14 Jul 1949. He married JEANIE MOORE.

Daniel Wayne Roeber and Jeanie Moore had the following children:

    i.   BLAKE[6] ROEBER was born in Apr 1978.

ii.   KENNETH LEIGH ROEBER was born on 07 Dec 1979.

146.   **LUANNE[5] ROEBER** (Jeanette Lucille[4] Weinert, Elsa Lucille[3] Neathery, Annie Lee[2] Edwards, William Archibald[1] Edwards) was born on 05 Dec 1952. She married **STEVEN SCHUETZE**.

Steven Schuetze and Luanne Roeber had the following children:

    i.   JOSEPH ROEBER[6] SCHUETZE was born on 26 May 1976.

    ii.   DENA SCHUETZE was born on 30 Aug 1978.

147.   **PATRICIA ANN[5] WEISE** (Annie Lee[4] Weinert, Elsa Lucille[3] Neathery, Annie Lee[2] Edwards, William Archibald[1] Edwards) was born on 24 May 1947. She married **EDWARD HAGEN**.

Edward Hagen and Patricia Ann Weise had the following children:

    i.   LEIGHAN[6] HAGEN was born on 30 Aug 1969.

    ii.   JASON HAGEN was born on 14 Oct 1974.

148.   **CHARLES EUGENE[5] CARTER** (Charles Clarence[4], Dorothy[3] Lester, Willie Maud[2] Edwards, William Archibald[1] Edwards) was born on 05 Oct 1952 in Dallas, Texas. He married Debra Elaine Meritt on 9 Jan 1981 in Tarrant County, Texas. She was born in 1960 in Texas.

More About Charles Eugene Carter:
Occupation: Dentist

More About Debra Elaine Meritt:
Occupation: Office Manager

Charles Eugene Carter and Debra Elaine Meritt had the following child:

    i.   LAUREN MICHELLE[6] CARTER was born on 27 Sep 1985 in Dallas, Dallas County, Texas.

149.   **MARCELLENE SNORF[5] WILSON** (John Franklin[4], William Henry[3], Carrie Louise[2] Edwards, William Archibald[1] Edwards) was born on 02 Dec 1946 in Dallas County, Texas. She married **STEPHEN HUNT SANDS**.

Stephen Hunt Sands and Marcellene Snorf Wilson had the following children:

    i.   WILSON LOYD[6] SANDS was born on 28 Sep 1970 in Dallas County, Texas.

    ii.   LOWELL HUNT SANDS was born on 18 Aug 1973 in Dallas County, Texas.

    iii.   STEPHEN STORM SANDS was born on 15 Sep 1976 in Dallas County, Texas.

    iv.   JOHN BOWMER SANDS was born on 27 Nov 1977 in Dallas County, Texas.

150.   **DAVID SNORF[5] WILSON** (John Franklin[4], William Henry[3], Carrie Louise[2] Edwards, William Archibald[1] Edwards) was born on 19 Apr 1954 in Dallas County, Texas. He married **DEBORAH LINDA FRY**.

David Snorf Wilson and Deborah Linda Fry had the following children:

    i.   SARA ANNE[6] WILSON was born on 15 Dec 1980 in Brazos County, Texas.

    ii.   STEVEN SNORF WILSON was born on 05 Jul 1984 in Smith County, Texas.

iii.　Frances Elizabeth Wilson was born on 28 Oct 1988 in Smith County, Texas.

151.　Ben Jones[5] Woodson (Ben Jones[4], Marjory Ruth[3] Jones, Mattie Elizabeth[2] Edwards, William Archibald[1] Edwards) was born on 10 Sep 1956 in Brownwood, Texas. He married Sharyn Kay Finegan.

Ben Jones Woodson and Sharyn Kay Finegan had the following children:

i.　Kara Leigh[6] Woodson was born on 28 May 1989 in Harris county, Texas.

ii.　Coulter Keyes Woodson was born on 18 Sep 1991 in Harris county, Texas.

152.　Laurilyn Louise[5] Woodson (Ben Jones[4], Marjory Ruth[3] Jones, Mattie Elizabeth[2] Edwards, William Archibald[1] Edwards) was born on 18 Jan 1959 in Del Norte, Colorado. She married Steven Wayne Builta.

Steven Wayne Builta and Laurilyn Louise Woodson had the following children:

i.　Steven Drake[6] Builta was born on 16 Apr 1992 in Travis County, Texas.

ii.　Kimberly Tanner Builta was born on 29 Jun 1995 in Travis County, Texas.

Generation 6

153.　Earl Leon[6] Wingo (Lela Patricia[5] Connally, Robert Edwards[4] Connally, Clara Lillian[3] Edwards, Theophilus Ambrose[2] Edwards, William Archibald[1] Edwards) was born on 22 Oct 1948 in Andalusia, Alabama. He married Candice Johnson on 14 Dec 1974.

Earl Leon Wingo and Candice Johnson had the following child:

i.　Jennifer Eiron[7] Wingo was born on 04 Apr 1977.

154.　Lloyd Daniel[6] Lewellen (Carol Joy[5] Cofer, William Frank[4] Cofer, Edna Cora[3] Skillern, Mary James Cora[2] Edwards, William Archibald[1] Edwards) was born on 11 Aug 1967 in Dallas County, Texas. He married Joni Sue Hammer. She was born on 08 Dec 1967.

Lloyd Daniel Lewellen and Joni Sue Hammer had the following children:

i.　Brianna Faith[7] Lewellen was born on 08 Jul 1996 in Dallas County, Texas.

ii.　Lauren Nicole Lewellen was born on 25 Oct 1989 in Dallas County, Texas.

155.　Kellie Rene[6] Tiner (Carol Sue[5] Lankford, Evelyn Faye[4] Alexander, Fay Edwina[3] Neathery, Annie Lee[2] Edwards, William Archibald[1] Edwards) was born on 19 Nov 1962 in Dallas, Texas. She married (1) Gregg Emmanuel Turner, son of Baxter Turner and Bobbie Roberts on 02 Apr 1984 in Longview, Texas. He was born on 25 Dec 1962 in Mesquite, Texas. She married Kenneth Ray Segers. He was born on 28 Apr 1962.

Gregg Emmanuel Turner and Kellie Rene Tiner had the following children:

i.　Jonathan Michael[7] Turner was born on 28 Apr 1986.

More About Jonathan Michael Turner: Military
Service: United States Marine Corps

ii.　Jessica Leigh Turner was born on 16 Nov 1988.

156.　Leslie Carol[6] Oates (John Richard[5], John Richard[4], Deron Adelle[3] Neathery, Annie Lee[2]

Edwards, William Archibald[1] Edwards) was born on 02 Mar 1967 in Lubbock, Texas. She married **ROBERT ERNEST ANDERSON**. He was born on 12 Sep 1965 in McLennan County, Texas.

Robert Ernest Anderson and Leslie Carol Oates had the following child:

    i.   AUSTIN BARRETT[7] ANDERSON was born on 15 Jul 1993 in Lubbock County, Texas.